THE TEN DAY OUTLINE

A WRITER'S GUIDE TO PLANNING A NOVEL IN TEN DAYS

LEWIS JORSTAD

THE
NOVEL
SMITHY

The Ten Day Outline: A Writer's Guide to Planning a Novel in Ten Days

Copyright © 2019 Lewis Jorstad

The Ten Day Novelist — Book One

Published by The Novel Smithy, LLC.

Printed in the United States of America.

1st Edition, 2019

ISBN (print): 978-1-7332079-0-4

ISBN (digital): 978-1-7332079-1-1

https://thenovelsmithy.com/

❀ Created with Vellum

"A goal without a plan is just a wish."

ANTOINE DE SAINT-EXUPÉRY, FRENCH WRITER
AND POET

CONTENTS

Join the Library!   vii
Where It All Begins   ix
Your Questions   xiii

1. Day One: Start With the Basics   1
2. Day Two: Finding Inspiration   17
3. Day Three: Exploring Every Angle   26
4. Day Four: The Start of Your Story's Scenes   36
5. Day Five: Forming a Scene Timeline   49
6. Day Six: Creating the Character Sheet   61
7. Day Seven: Six Elements of Structure   85
8. Day Eight: Where It All Comes Together   104
9. Day Nine: Completing the Picture   114
10. Day Ten: What About Tomorrow?   131

What Comes Next?   139
Join the Library!   141
About the Author   143
The Complete Ten Day Outlining Process   145
Also by Lewis Jorstad   153

JOIN THE LIBRARY!

Ever wish there was a library of resources built just for novelists? Well, guess what—there is!

Check out the **Novel Smithy Resource Library** and grab your **FREE Character Creation Workbook**.

https://thenovelsmithy.com/library/

WHERE IT ALL BEGINS

Nearly all aspiring authors will face a similar struggle—they want to write a novel, but they don't know where to begin.

It's undeniable that such a project is a major undertaking. Not only do you need to build a story, but then you need to populate it with a meaningful cast of characters and conflicts. Creating these elements is a huge task in its own right—not to mention writing your story as well!

Unfortunately, far too many writers never reach the writing stage at all.

You see, not only is writing a novel intimidating, but it's complex. Your story will dictate how you create your characters, but without characters to live and act in your story, how do you know how the journey begins? Worse still, you may know exactly *what* needs to happen in your novel, but you're at a loss for ideas on *how* to make it happen.

When faced with these difficult realities, many writers simply give up, while others put off writing their novel for so long that they lose the drive to write at all. This unfortunate reality marks the end of the road for far too many writers.

However, there's a remedy to this problem: outlining.

While the word "outline" might bring up visions of bulleted lists and school essays, a truly well-built outline—one designed specifically with a novel in mind—goes far beyond these.

Before ever sitting down to write your first draft, creating an outline lets you add depth to your ideas and discover unique ways to expand on your story. It gives you a bird's-eye view of your novel, helping you weave all of its elements together into something cohesive and meaningful. Most importantly, your outline becomes a roadmap, guiding you past writer's block, comforting you when you doubt your story's potential, and encouraging you as you complete those final few chapters.

The simple power of a well-built, cohesive outline can't be understated.

Of course, for something to be so useful, it probably isn't the easiest to create. Your outline needs to do a few important things to help you prepare for writing your novel.

It should:

- Organize your ideas in a cohesive way.
- Provide critical details about your story.
- Give you space to brainstorm and experiment.
- Push you to explore every angle of your ideas.
- Come together quickly, before you lose the spark that got you excited to write in the first place.

This is why so many writers give up on their stories. Not

only is writing a novel intimidating in its own right, but planning and preparing for one is complex as well. Their core idea may be strong, but expanding that idea into a fully fledged story without anything or anyone to guide them is simply too much.

That's where this challenge comes in.

The Ten Day Outline is exactly what the name suggests—a ten-day challenge meant to guide you through every step of outlining and planning your novel. Even if you're starting with just a single idea, this challenge will help you build on that initial inspiration and expand it into a fully realized story, complete with a compelling cast of characters, scenes, and settings.

Thanks to a series of easy-to-follow goals, you won't have to wonder if you're missing something and you won't have to spend months struggling through a first draft you never had a plan for. By the end of this challenge, you'll be one step closer to becoming an author!

All you need are ten days and the passion to create a novel all your own.

YOUR QUESTIONS

How should I use this book?

Because this book is designed to be a step-by-step guide, you'll likely be referencing it a lot as you work on your outline. To try and make that process easier, I have a few tips and recommendations.

For starters, I encourage you to read each chapter and then complete its goals before moving on to later days. Every day of this challenge is designed to build towards the next, so you won't want to jump around out of order. By reading each chapter as you work on its goals, you should find the whole process is much more organized and easier to follow.

Of course, you may occasionally need a reminder of what your goals are for each day. In those instances, you can either flip to the goals at the end of each chapter or to The Complete Ten Day Outlining Process at the very back of the book.

How much time will I need to dedicate to the challenge?

To complete this challenge, you should only need to dedicate one or two hours each day to writing. However, there will be a few days later in the challenge that will require more time —specifically Days Seven and Eight. If possible, complete those days when you know you'll have extra time to spare.

Do I have to complete this challenge in ten consecutive days?

I strongly encourage you to complete this challenge in ten days. When at its best, outlining is a quick process meant to capture the original spark of inspiration that got you excited to write in the first place. As more and more time passes between days, you may find yourself losing steam.

Completing the challenge over ten consecutive days will also help immerse you in your story. You'll come up with new ideas while doing the dishes, driving to work, and walking the dog, simply because you've tuned your creative subconscious into your story.

While you can certainly split the challenge up if needed—life does get in the way, of course—your story will benefit the most from doing each day in order, one after the other.

Will this be difficult?

I won't lie to you—this is a challenge for a reason. Some of these days, especially the final few, will have you asking tough questions about the story you want to tell.

However, by the tenth day I'm confident that work will have paid off. After completing this process over and over while testing and iterating on it, I can't say I've reached Day Ten a single time and still had reservations about the story I had just created.

What if I've already started my first draft?

No problem! You may have a head start on some of your goals, but the end result will be the same. You should still plan to complete the full ten-day challenge from start to finish in order to get the most out of it.

What if I'm writing a series?

In the case of a series, there are a few ways to approach this challenge. Perhaps the easiest is to complete all ten days for each book you plan to write, just like you would if they were standalone novels. However, this is also the longest route.

Personally, I prefer to complete Days One through Four with my entire series in mind, treating it as if it was one massive book. From there, you can easily finish the challenge for each individual novel you plan to write, using your work from Days One through Four as a foundation.

Is there anything I need to know before I start?

This book is designed with beginners in mind, so I'll do my best to explain basic terms and information when necessary. However, having an understanding of common storytelling concepts like story structure and character development will make a big difference in how your outline ultimately turns out.

However, since I won't have space to explain every detail, I've created a few free resources on story structure and character creation that you can check out here:

https://thenovelsmithy.com/library/

If you're unfamiliar with either of these concepts, I strongly encourage you to check those resources out. They'll make a big difference in how comfortable you are with many of the goals found in later chapters, and will make this challenge easier overall.

Will I need anything else before I start this challenge?

Other than having time in your schedule, all you need is yourself!

DAY ONE: START WITH THE BASICS

AN IDEA IS at the center of every great story in human history, and if you're hoping to write a novel of your own, I imagine it's because you already have an idea in mind.

Many of the writers I've met have so many ideas that they don't know where to start. They have drawers full of notebooks, each with the beginnings of a novel scribbled on the first few pages. Others have lists and binders full of bullet points chronicling random snippets of scenes and characters. Personally, I'm in so deep that I have both—and it takes up quite a lot of space in my tiny apartment.

Of course, that may not be the case for you.

Even if you have an idea of how to start your story, you'll likely run into goals throughout this challenge that stump you. There's a reason humanity's creative muse is portrayed as a fickle lover, blessing us with their presence one moment before abandoning us the next. Every artist, writers included, will find themselves in a rut and out of ideas at some point.

However, if you want to complete this challenge, you can't

leave yourself beholden to your muse. While you may find it helpful to step away for an hour or two when you get stuck, I discourage you from pausing for multiple days or weeks because of writer's block. Trust me, I've done it before, and more likely than not you'll never get back to writing.

This is why Day One is all about getting you into the right mindset for this challenge.

Specifically, we'll be working through an intensive method designed to help you break through writer's block no matter when you face it. You'll also decide on the core idea of your story and I'll show you how to frame it as a premise. Finally, before the day is over, we'll set up the beginnings of your outline!

Calling on Your Muse

The process we're about to go through is meant to jumpstart your inspiration whenever you run out of ideas. If you're starting this challenge unsure what to write about, this should solve that problem.

Of course, you may already be bursting with inspiration, in which case you're welcome to skip to writing your premise below. However, keep this section in your back pocket, because you may find it comes in handy later on. While I've framed it as a way to come up with story ideas, this method will be just as useful for progressing your plot or creating characters in future days.

To start, all you need is a few sheets of paper and a pen—you won't want to erase your work during this process. Find a space where you can focus and turn on some relaxing music.

Your goal here is to write down a list of fifty ideas, events, memories, or experiences from your life. On the surface, that may sound like a lot, so I understand if you're taken aback by that number. However, stick with me for now and push yourself to find unique things to write.

A great place to start is with your own life:

- What strange experiences have you had?
- What are you afraid of?
- Who is your best friend and how did you meet?
- What is your strongest or most impactful memory?
- What do you want to achieve in life?
- What would you consider a great adventure?

As you get deeper into your list, you'll find yourself letting go of your subconscious restrictions. This is the benefit of writing so many individual ideas—you're forcing your mind to think outside its normal limits.

During this process, you may also be drawn to historical tidbits you find fascinating or snippets of conversation you overheard at the grocery store. Write those down as well! You can even use song lyrics, quotes from movies or books, or entire subplots from stories you know and love. While that might feel like plagiarism on the surface, you'll soon be remixing these ideas into something new. At this stage, there's nothing wrong with using other's work as fodder for your inspiration. Of course, don't shy away from unique ideas of your own that come up during this process either.

Once you hit a solid fifty ideas, sit back, rest your hands, and look over what you've written down. In all likelihood, you'll start to notice a pattern. Did you focus on relationships or dear friends? Were you caught up in childhood adventures, fairytales, and travel? Or did you ignore your childhood in favor of accomplishments from later in life, or from the lives of those you admire?

No matter what your focus was, you'll probably find that it matches the books you already read—or are trying to write. If you're a big fantasy geek like I am, it'll feel natural to focus on ideas related to history and ancient worlds. Romance readers will probably write about relationships, and western lovers may focus on exploration or discovery.

Of course, this isn't always true.

This process has a way of revealing things about yourself you may not have expected. For instance, last time I created one of these lists I ended up with an idea for a cyberpunk novel in the vein of *Ghost in the Shell*, despite not being a huge science fiction reader—which is a long way of saying that, if you find your list taking strange turns you didn't expect, follow it. You may discover interests you never knew you had!

Mixing and Matching

Now that you have your list in hand, it's time to get creative. Take a moment to review what you've written down and ask yourself: are there any common themes or subjects?

Based on the patterns you find, you should be able to identify a few prospective genres. For instance, if you wrote a lot about recent news or international travel, a spy thriller may be calling to you.

Of course, like I mentioned above, you'll probably be drawn to genres you already read, but don't limit yourself. If you're a hardcore action reader but find yourself drifting towards fantasy, there's nothing wrong with that—and the same goes for literary fiction. You may feel deeply attached to the classics, but if your ideas are pointing elsewhere, it's worth exploring them. After all, just because your list skews towards one genre or another, doesn't mean those same ideas can't apply to your favorite genre in interesting ways.

Here are some common genres and their themes, though feel free to explore options not on this list:

- **Fantasy:** adventure, history, fairytales, magic
- **Science Fiction:** technology, space, exploration, adventure
- **Romance:** relationships, love, betrayal, family
- **Westerns:** history, nature, discovery, past technologies
- **Mysteries:** crime, law enforcement, government, human psychology
- **Thrillers:** espionage, international travel, crime, human psychology
- **Horror:** human psychology, dreams, crime, death
- **Literary Novels:** human psychology, social systems, death, history

Once you've reviewed your list, pick one or two genres, either based on what you wrote down or on the genre you most want to write in. With your list and genres in mind, it's time to begin the matching process.

To do this, scan through your list and consider how these individual ideas could come together into a unique story, using your chosen genres as guidance. You may pick small elements from multiple ideas and pair them together, or remix entire bullet points with inspiration you gained from creating your list. Throughout this process, your genres should serve as a loose framework, telling you where your ideas could go.

Finally, after going through all fifty items on your list, you should have created at least five potential story ideas (if not one or two more).

What's so great about this is that none of the individual things you wrote down are likely to produce a novel on their own. However, when combined with others, you create something with much more depth. Plus, by having five different options you not only get to pick the best of the bunch, but you can mix and match those ideas too, creating something even more unique. That's why plagiarism wasn't a concern when coming up with your list. Even if you ripped a core idea straight from *The Adventures of Sherlock Holmes*, by blending it with your personal experiences studying abroad and your love of romantic dramas, you've turned it into something new.

Let's look at some examples:

———

My Potential List:

- When I was a toddler, I crawled out of my crib and hid under the bed. No one found me for two hours.
- In my favorite movie, the lead character travels to China to save a man who was wrongfully arrested.
- My parents couldn't tell me much about their jobs because they worked for the government.
- In Scottish legends, the fairy folk steal unbaptized children and replace them with changelings who later die of an unknown illness.

Prospective Genres:

- Thriller
- Fantasy

Possible Story Ideas:

- After sneaking out of the house, a young child is abducted into a fantasy world.
- Growing up, the main character's parents were foreign spies. When they're arrested for treason, he'll have to decide whether to save them or not.
- The main character is a new mother when her baby disappears. Two decades later she sees her daughter, now grown, walking down the street. She's certain the woman is her child.
- A family adopts a young girl thinking they're a normal teen, but they're secretly a foreign operative sent as a spy during the Cold War.

———

These resulting story ideas—even when based on a short list —are fairly diverse. Each has its own unique twist, which is exactly what you're looking for. Just imagine the variety of stories you could create with a list of fifty ideas to play with!

As I mentioned previously, this method isn't limited to story ideas either. In fact, you can use it to overcome writer's block no matter where you are in the writing process.

For instance, you may be trying to write your story's final battle, but don't know how to progress. Pause and go through this method, only instead of choosing a genre, think about how you could incorporate your list into your existing story. The process is the same, but your focus is slightly different. Instead of Scottish legends and a missing kid coming together into a plot about foreign agents, it could just as easily become a big reveal where your hero isn't the villain's child after all.

What's so powerful about this method is that you're opening your mind to new ideas without concern for how relevant they are, how good they might be, or even if they're complete sentences. Without those mental barriers, your inspiration can flow more freely and you become less constrained by writer's block.

Of course, I'll be the first to admit that it's easy to buy into the romantic ideal that great novels are created thanks to miraculous blessings from an author's muse. Anything less isn't novel worthy, right?

Not so.

A unique idea has just as much potential whether it came from a dream, a stroke of genius, or a purposeful process like this one. The quality of your story is up to the unique twists and turns you create, not the origins of your ideas. Even the most prolific authors aren't always in their muses' good graces, and they each have systems of their own to stay inspired.

Inspiration plays an important role in many stages of the writing process, but it'll only be there if you invite it to the party first.

A High-Concept Idea

At this point, you should have a clear idea of the novel you want to write, whether you started with that idea or created it through the process above. Now it's time to turn that idea into a premise and begin building your draft outline.

The question is, what exactly is a premise?

In the publishing world, your premise acts as the unique bit of your story that gets readers invested in your novel. It's the basis of the blurb on your back cover, and it's what you'll pitch to readers, agents, friends, and family members when you tell them you're writing a book. Perhaps more importantly though, your premise will be the one to two sentence synopsis that forms the foundation of your story. It will act as your guiding star when you're writing, so it's one of the first things you'll need to begin your outline.

However, before creating your premise you'll need to make sure you've expanded your core idea enough to turn it into a premise at all.

Your premise needs to fulfill a few criteria to work:

- It should imply a conflict,
- It should show a unique perspective,
- It should tease how your story will start,
- And it should hint at your main character's reaction to the conflict.

Essentially, it needs to be high-concept.

The term high-concept comes from the world of Hollywood screenplays, where it's used to describe movies with a high box-office potential. Yet it's just as applicable to any other type of story. A high-concept idea is one that's unique, immediately intriguing, driven by a clear conflict, and easy to sum up in a short pitch.

Many writers will obsess over making sure their idea is high-concept, and that's certainly admirable, especially since high-concept ideas are what most publishers and readers are looking for. However—and this is a *big* however—don't get too caught up by this step. You're early in the outlining process, and we'll be returning to your premise in later chapters anyway. Instead, this is your chance to flesh out your idea until it loosely fits the requirements above.

For example, let's take one of the story ideas I created earlier and make it high-concept:

- A family adopts a young girl thinking they're a normal teen, but they're secretly a foreign operative sent as a spy during the Cold War.

This is in a good place as far as initial ideas go, but I haven't implied a clear conflict quite yet. Yes, the main character is a spy, but for all we know that never causes much trouble.

To make this idea high-concept, I need to expand on it by asking a few questions:

- What is this idea's unique twist?
- Does this idea encourage further questions?
- Does this idea hint at a main character and setting?
- Is there a clear conflict, and what is that conflict?
- Does this idea imply a goal for the main character?

After considering these questions, my new idea might look something like this:

- A young teenager is on an assignment from a foreign government. As part of that assignment, they're sent to be adopted by a family of special agents. From

> there, they secretly pass along information about
> their new parents and siblings to their superiors.

Much better! Not only does this imply a clear conflict between the main character and their adopted family, but it adds a unique spin. Instead of being adopted into any old family, they've been sent to live with a family of opposing spies. It's easy to imagine how this story could develop, twist, and turn—exactly what we're looking for.

You should apply this same set of questions to your own idea. Write down what you have so far and check it against the requirements we discussed above—is there a clear conflict, a unique perspective, and an idea of how your story begins? If not, look closer at how you can expand on your idea.

You'll hopefully find this isn't too difficult, however, it's still possible you'll hit a sticking point. This means you simply need to return to the brainstorming process from the start of the chapter. Explore some potential options that could make your idea high-concept, specifically focusing on conflicts for your story. Once you're happy with what you've come up with, you're ready to move on.

Forming Your Premise

Like we talked about above, your premise is a one to two sentence synopsis of your entire novel. It'll encapsulate your story's conflict, your main character, and their initial goal. Fortunately, creating a premise isn't too difficult once you have a strong idea to work with.

Here are a few famous examples:

- **Mulan:** A young woman disguises herself as a man in order to join the Chinese army and protect her father from the draft, entering a deadly war in the process.
- **How to Train Your Dragon:** A young Viking captures a dragon, but when he fails to kill it it ends up becoming his best friend. Now the two must fight to convince his society that dragons aren't the enemies they thought they were.
- **Princess Mononoke:** A young warrior is cursed by a demon while trying to protect his village, and must set out on a journey to find a cure. In the process, he'll find himself at the center of a war between humanity and nature.
- **Star Wars:** A young Jedi goes on a quest to destroy an evil empire, only to discover that his father is one of its leaders, betraying everything he believes.

And here's the premise for the idea we've been developing:

- During the Cold War, a teenaged girl sets out as an undercover agent to spy on their adoptive family—a difficult mission, considering their adoptive parents are spies themselves.

You'll notice that none of these are particularly specific, that they're all limited to one or two sentences long, and that there are no character names or clearly defined scenes. That's on purpose.

Remember, your premise only needs three things: a main character, a goal for that character, and a conflict.

This is because your premise is just the framework for the rest of your story. As you continue developing your outline your ideas will evolve and change, and you want your premise to allow for that. However, by defining a strong premise from the start, you prevent yourself from wandering too far off course and creating scenes and characters that have no connection back to your main story.

Basically, your premise gives you the best of both worlds—plenty of room to experiment, but enough structure that you'll always know the foundation of your novel.

So, take a moment to sift through your high-concept idea and boil it down into one or two sentences, making sure you end up with a main character, their initial goal, and the conflict they'll face. This will be your premise.

Beginning The Draft Outline

Though setting up your outline is your main goal for today, this will probably be the quickest task you complete—which might be nice, especially after figuring out your story's premise!

This early version of your outline will be called the "draft outline", acting as a record of the ideas you develop throughout this challenge. Later on it'll grow and become a more important tool, until we eventually turn it into your Master Outline. While your draft outline is a place to jot down notes, explore random ideas, and indulge in some brainstorming, your Master Outline will be the roadmap you eventually use to write your novel. However, that won't come until the end of the challenge—for now, your draft outline will be all you need.

To start your draft outline, you'll first need to decide where to create it. Personally, I like the ease and organization of writing on a computer, but you may prefer the analog feel of pen and paper. Regardless of your preferred medium, consider these factors:

———

Ease Of Use:

Your outline should let you create lists, mark changes, and jot down notes. You'll also want to consider how you'll include images and other media. In a binder or notebook, this is fairly straightforward—you can simply clip all of your materials into the rings and move them around as needed. For digital formats, consider keeping everything together on a single USB drive or in a well-labeled folder.

You should also take into account how you'll protect your work from damage. This could include anything from computer failure to a spilled glass of water, so make sure you keep your work in a safe place (and if possible, create multiple backups, just in case).

Level of Distraction:

This is mostly a warning for the digital crowd—myself included—but even pen and paper can distract you, and you'll want to avoid these distractions whenever possible.

Instead of using the notebook you keep your grocery list in, use one dedicated only to your novel. Likewise, approach digital writing with caution. If you're the type of person who is easily distracted by email or the Internet, make sure you limit those distractions before you use your computer for this challenge.

Enjoyment:

If you hate your handwriting or get hand cramps, you won't

enjoy outlining on paper. In the same vein, if your resolution for the year is to limit your screen time, don't outline your novel on a laptop.

Additionally, whatever your chosen medium ends up being, make sure you understand how to use it well—especially if it's a program or other software—and will look forward to working with it.

———

Once you've decided what to work with, beginning your draft outline is as simple as writing down your premise at the top of a blank document. With that done, you've officially completed Day One!

By now, your draft outline should have:

- **Your one to two sentence premise**

By now, your draft outline might have:

- **Notes about your original inspiration**
- **A longer paragraph describing your full, high-concept idea**

The Goals of Day One

Despite how short your draft outline is at this point, you've gotten a lot done.

Developing a strong premise from the beginning may seem trivial at first—I did say we would revisit your premise later on, and we still have nine days left in this challenge. However, your premise is the bedrock of your novel. By finding any weaknesses in it now, you'll have a much smoother challenge ahead of you, and a much better novel in your future.

Tomorrow we'll begin cultivating your inspiration, but for now, here are the goals you've completed for Day One:

1. Brainstorm an initial idea, either using one you already have or creating one for this challenge.
2. Expand on your initial idea until it fulfills the four requirements of a high-concept story.
3. Condense your idea into a one to two sentence premise that clearly outlines your main character, their initial goal, and your story's conflict.
4. Pick a medium and begin your draft outline by writing your new premise at the top.

On to Day Two!

2

DAY TWO: FINDING INSPIRATION

DESPITE BEING SUCH AN AVID READER, I'm mostly a visual learner. If I can watch a video or see a diagram of something, I'm not only more likely to remember it, but more likely to understand it as well. When I read a great novel, I don't see words on the page as much as a movie playing out in my head. There's a reason you'll find more and more images as we get into later, more difficult chapters.

Knowing the type of learner you are is important for your own novel as well. When you think about your story, what do you see?

If you're as visual as I am, then I imagine we share a similar experience—you see a movie playing behind your eyelids. Of course, you may be more musically inclined, or maybe a series of words really is how you envision your story.

There's really no right or wrong here, so before we get into today's goals, take a moment to consider what kinds of media you're most drawn to—images, music, words, a mix of all three, or something else entirely.

Today will be all about cultivating a collection of this chosen media, designed to spark your imagination and get you into the world of your story. Music will help you feel the mood of a scene. Images will help you imagine a setting, while quotes might echo the voice of a future character. Even videos might come into play!

Ultimately, regardless of the type of media you collect, these supporting materials will not only be helpful, but essential as you create scenes, settings, and characters later on.

Creating Your Collection

At this point in the challenge, you should have a single core idea—your premise—and potentially some scenes and characters to go with it. Today, you'll begin expanding that idea by bringing in outside inspiration to add depth and substance to your story.

Would this landscape make a good setting for my hero's home planet? Does this piece of music match the tone I want for an intense final battle? Asking these sorts of questions will stretch your story from a single vision into a network of potential ideas.

To start this process, you'll need to gather different pieces of media en masse, with your goal being to create a collection of at least one hundred items.

While this may sound like a lot at first glance, you should have a wide variety to choose from. Your collection might contain images, music, movie clips, quotes, poems, excerpts from other stories, or even diagrams—basically anything you can think of. You're even welcome to sketch a few pictures of your own!

However, you don't want to simply gather up anything you come across. Each piece of media you collect needs to be relevant to the story you want to tell. This is why you created your premise yesterday—you'll need to keep it in mind as you conduct your search, so make sure it's handy.

Of course, that raises the question of how you'll find this media and where you'll keep it. Personally, I think a computer makes the most sense for this. The Internet gives you access to anything you could imagine, and you can easily save most things to a folder on your desktop. This is especially true if your draft outline is already digital.

However, I still encourage you to use a computer even if you're outlining in a binder or notebook. Later on you may choose to print out images or add quotes directly to your outline, but for now, gather your chosen media digitally. We'll be revisiting it again in a few moments.

With that said, you can begin searching.

This process will inevitably take some time, but I encourage you to limit yourself to two hours. This will not only keep you focused, but it'll prevent you from falling down the rabbit hole that is the Internet—something far too easy to do. Instead of searching for the absolute best photo of a neon lit city for thirty minutes, give yourself permission to find four or five good images in a fraction of the time. Remember that we'll be returning to these materials in a few minutes, so they don't need to be perfect just yet.

You'll hopefully find this process moves quickly at first, since you should already have a mental image of at least a few elements of your story. This means you can base your search on what you already know:

- Are there any scenes or settings you have in mind?
- Are there real world locations you want to write about, or fictional ones that resemble real life?
- What does your hero or villain look like?
- What kind of tone will your novel have?

However, as your collection creeps closer to one hundred, you may start feeling stuck. You don't want to gather a ton of duplicate material—ten photos of a snowy tree might be too many—so what do you do?

Well, for starters, being stuck here is a good thing. It means you're pushing your ideas beyond their current boundaries and discovering new and interesting ways to expand your story. Still, that doesn't help the frustration this causes, especially when you don't want to waste a ton of time during your two-hour limit.

So, here are some prompts to help you move forward:

- Where does your main character live?
- What does their home look like?
- What does your main character look like?
- What does your villain look like?
- Does your main character have any allies?
- Are there common plants or animals in this world?
- Does your main character have any pets or animal companions?
- What type of work does your main character do?
- What tools would they use for that work?
- What type of technology is common in this world?
- What type of clothing is in fashion?
- What types of food are common in this world?
- Are there different social classes, tribes, nations, or races in your story?

- Are there any special symbols to consider, such as religious or social icons?
- Will your main character ever travel to new places, and what will they look like?
- Does your main character have a special talisman or item they carry with them?
- Are there any monsters or creatures in this world?
- Where will the final showdown take place?
- What is the tone of your story—dark, moody, uplifting, playful, et cetera?
- Is there a MacGuffin or other item your characters are fighting over?

It's possible you won't have answers for some of these questions just yet, or that they may not apply to your story at all. That's ok! You'll get to explore these questions and others like them later on, so for now, they're simply here to help inspire you.

Once you reach one hundred items or hit two hours—whichever comes first—you've finished this phase. Time to start sorting.

The Sorting Phase

When you begin the sorting phase, you should have a large mass of different media stored in one common place. That's certainly helpful, but for these items to be truly beneficial you'll want to curate them.

Fortunately, this step is fairly simple—all you need to do is go through your collection and separate them into common categories that can be as generic or specific as you'd like. Personally, I like to do this using separate folders on my desktop. Here are some categories to consider:

- Settings
- Characters
- Tools and Objects
- Plants and Animals
- Culture

Of course, you'll probably end up tweaking these to fit your specific story. You may have a folder dedicated to your main character, and it could include photos of what they look like, clips of music that represents their personality, or images of their home. Even if you use the generic categories above, make sure they feel intuitive to you. You'll be referencing these categories a lot over the next few days, so having them organized will be a huge relief.

This also extends to what you put in each category. As you gathered items, you should have begun forming a clearer vision of your story. Your old ideas may have changed, with new ideas taking their place. This means your current collection could end up with a lot of extra "stuff" if you're not careful. Therefore, the last part of the sorting phase is to remove this extraneous "stuff" from your final collection.

You want your categories to be bite-sized representations of the various places, people, objects, and events you hope to explore in your story—essentially a curated museum of your inspiration. They should all have a similar tone and feel, because you're trying to create a cohesive story. Leaving excess media will only make it harder to reference your collection down the road.

So, before moving on, browse through the collection you've created and consider each item you've included. Does it still fit with your vision of your story? If not, send it to the recycling bin.

Returning to Your Outline

By now, you've hopefully developed a clearer picture of where your novel is going. Even if you already had a strong sense of your story when you started this challenge, creating a curated collection of media always results in a few new ideas being added to the mix.

This means your final task for today is to make a record of those new ideas. Whether you completely rethought your story's direction or just tweaked a few elements, you'll still want to write down how your story has evolved. Yesterday, your draft outline only had your premise at the top, so now is your opportunity to add the extra details.

Skipping to a line below your premise, write a few notes describing your story. What happens, where does it take place, who is involved, and where do they go? Again, you may not have answers to all of these, or your answers may still be vague, but that's ok. There's no need to go into tons of detail quite yet.

Of course, this may leave you wondering—what about the collection you just created? How does that fit into your draft outline?

The answer to this is largely up to you, but here's my recommendation: leave your collection on its own for now, especially if you're outlining on paper.

While you're more than welcome to print out images and quotes if you'd like to, keeping it digital will not only save you printer ink, but it'll preserve your collection in an easy-to-use format. Digital simply makes the most sense for this step. However, even if you're already outlining on your computer, keeping your collection separate will likely be the best choice for now—and this is especially true since your draft outline will undergo a major overhaul at the end of this challenge.

So, for now, keep your collection in a dedicated folder on an USB drive or backed up in some other form.

By now, your draft outline should have:

- Your one to two sentence premise
- **A short list covering the basics of your story**

By now, your draft outline might have:

- Notes about your original inspiration
- A longer paragraph describing your full, high-concept idea

The Goals of Day Two

While it may seem trivial to spend two hours wandering around the Internet in search of pictures of trees, castles, and spaceship, I want to give you an idea of how important this collection will be—and not just for this challenge.

If you think of your novel as a house, then you know it needs a few basic parts: a foundation, a roof, walls, et cetera. Your premise is your novel's foundation, and later on we'll be building the other structural elements that'll hold your story together.

However, even a structurally perfect house would be barren without something inside it. That's why today was all about developing your novel's personality. Just like a house needs paint, furniture, and someone to live there, your collection will help you add the places, characters, and colors that bring your story's world to life.

Most importantly, this collection will do more than help you create a better outline.

When you go to write your first draft, your outline and your collection will be there to serve as blueprints for your story. Specifically, your collection will be there to spark your imagination when the right words don't come to you, when you've forgotten how a scene feels, or when you've lost touch with the settings and characters you've created. Through your collection, you can reorient yourself with the places and people of your novel, even in the face of the most severe writer's block—and that's a very valuable thing.

Tomorrow we'll push your premise to its limit, but for now, here are the goals you've completed for Day Two:

1. Gather 100 pieces of media (images, music, quotes, excerpts, et cetera...) that represent your story.
2. Separate this media into categories of your choice.
3. Sort through these categories and remove any items that no longer fit your story.
4. Write down your current vision of your story, along with any new ideas you've come up with.

On to Day Three!

DAY THREE: EXPLORING EVERY ANGLE

WHEN I FIRST BEGAN WRITING, I was the worst at following through on my stories. Today is about making sure you don't repeat my same mistakes.

Sure, I had plenty of ideas—you might remember the pile of notebooks I mentioned on Day One—but I always seemed to lose momentum a few chapters into my novels. It took a long time and many abandoned stories for me to realize why this was the case.

Fortunately, with the benefit of hindsight, I now know that I simply wasn't pushing my stories to their limit. I stuck too closely to my original ideas, never branching out or experimenting, and I ran out of inspiration as a result. Whenever I hit roadblocks while writing, my understanding of my story was too fragile to survive.

At this point in the challenge, you're probably in this same place. You have a solid premise, but you don't necessarily have an expansive story to support it. So far, your primary focus has been on getting your mind into the groove of your

\ story and developing a mental picture of where it might go. Many writers would stop there, but if my experience is anything to go by, that's not enough. It's time for your focus to shift, and for you to start exploring the many possibilities of your premise.

Your First Round of Questions

First things first—pull out your draft outline.

You'll want to start today by going back over the notes you wrote down yesterday. Your first official goal for today will be to brainstorm a series of ten questions based on those notes. These should be personal to your story, and should dig into any elements that are still unknown.

Below are some examples, but I wouldn't rely only on these. You'll want to adapt your questions to your specific idea, so add as many original ones as you can—especially if you already know the answer to a few of the ones below:

- Who is my main character, where do they come from, and why are they here now?
- How will this character get involved in my story?
- How will this character react to my story's conflict?
- Why is this conflict happening in the first place?
- Who feels the effects of this conflict?
- How will they react?
- Who or what is my villain?
- Why is my villain involved?
- What is my villain's stake in this conflict?
- What is one truly unique aspect of my story?

If you get on a roll while brainstorming and end up with more than ten questions, that's perfectly ok! Don't limit yourself to ten, but make sure you hit that number. After all, your goal here is to thoroughly work through any holes in your story. Once you write each question in your draft outline, skip five or more lines beneath it, because you'll be answering these in just a moment.

Now, remember the premise I created back on Day One?

- During the Cold War, a teenaged girl sets out as an undercover agent to spy on their adoptive family—a difficult mission, considering their adoptive parents are spies themselves.

Here are some questions I could ask based on that premise:

- What government is my main character working for, and why?
- Why was this specific family a target? Aren't there plenty of other spies out there?
- What secret is my main character trying to find?
- What'll be the consequence of them finding this secret or failing to find it?
- Will they have a change of heart, or will this family always be an enemy?

You'll notice that I've tailored all of these questions to the premise I created above. They specifically dive deeper into who my main character is, why they're in the situation they're in, and how the conflict of my story might progress.

Take a moment to do the same for your own premise. Once you've generated at least ten questions based on your story, it's time to explore possible answers.

Of course, it's not as simple as answering each question and moving on. You want to explore all the possibilities of your idea, so instead of creating a single answer, you'll be providing two. This is because, by answering each question twice, you force yourself to look past your immediate instincts. Your first answer will almost always be the most obvious one, and there's nothing wrong with that. However, by taking that answer off the table, you push your story into areas you may not have explored otherwise.

This is much like the mixing and matching process we talked about back on Day One. Each individual answer represents an individual idea. Once you have two written down, you can pick the bits and pieces you like from both of them. This means the final answers you create in the next step will be far stronger and more interesting than either of your initial answers were. Plus, this process helps you develop a stronger understanding of your story as a whole.

However, all this comes with a word of warning: you may get stuck trying to find answers.

If that happens, give yourself permission to step away for a moment. Go for a walk around the block, listen to a song or two, or clean your living room. Do something that allows your brain to space out—meaning no TV or social media. Personally, I like to make a snack or cook dinner, and for especially frustrating questions I'll even scrub a few dishes. Whatever your preferences may be, this short break should be all about opening yourself up to a more creative headspace, allowing your subconscious to work through the roadblocks you're facing.

Once you've written down two answers for each of your ten questions, you can continue on.

Going Deeper

As I said above, you shouldn't stop exploring your ideas after only one round of questioning. To truly create depth in your story—and prevent yourself from getting stuck later in the challenge—you'll want to go through a second set of questions that arise directly from the answers you just created.

Of course, that means you need to know which of your two answers is your favorite first. To do this, simply pull out a highlighter. After reading through each question and its corresponding answers, highlight the parts that stand out to you the most. These may be the most interesting or applicable to your story, or they may be the ones you're most excited to write about.

Once you've highlighted all of your favorite answers, take a moment to write these chosen sections below your original round of questions. If you highlighted entire answers, this is simple—just copy what you had written previously. On the other hand, if you mixed and matched elements from multiple sections, this may require more brain power, but it should still be fairly straightforward. Simply figure out how you can combine the highlighted pieces into a single, new answer, and record the result in your draft outline.

This is where you'll start your second round of questioning.

With your new set of ten answers written down, come up with another question based on each of them. To create these, think specifically about how you can further expand on each idea. You might also consider what information is still unknown or uncertain about your story.

While it's harder to create examples for this round—

especially since you should be tailoring your new questions to your specific answers—thinking about the six types of questions can help:

- Who is this happening to?
- What is happening?
- When is it happening?
- Where is it happening?
- How is it happening?
- Why is it happening—including why it's happening in this place, in this way, or at this time?

Of the six, I would argue that how and why are the most important, but all of these deserve some focus. By looking at your ten highlighted answers and considering these six options for each, you should start forming ideas for further questions.

Here's an example of how this process might go:

————

QUESTION #1: Why was this specific family a target? Aren't there plenty of other spy families out there?

- This family has access to critical state secrets related to the United States' nuclear program, and it's believed they have a stolen set of blueprints for the latest model of an American nuclear bomb.
- This family has a personal history with the leader of the Soviet KGB. Part of why they were chosen is this secret personal vendetta.

FINAL ANSWER: This family has access to the United

States' nuclear facilities, and the leader of the Soviet KGB also has a secret, personal vendetta against them.

QUESTION #2: Why does he have a vendetta against them?

- They were <u>fellow spies against Germany during WWII</u> and became close friends in the process, but when the Cold War began, the Americans <u>broke off ties with their Soviet friend</u>.
- The wife developed <u>a fake romantic relationship</u> with a Soviet man, who was then only a low-level spy, as a part of a mission at the start of the Cold War. When he found out it was all a ploy to get information, <u>he vowed to get revenge</u>.

FINAL ANSWER: They were fellow spies during WWII, and during their time together the wife developed a romantic relationship with the eventual leader of the Soviet KGB. However, when the Cold War began, she broke all ties with him and rejected him for being a Communist.

––––––

Notice how I have two sets of answers for each question, which I've then combined into a single, final answer. You should do the same for your own story. To do this, come up with two answers for each of the ten new questions you created previously. Then, highlight the pieces you like most and rewrite your final answers below.

Technically you could go through this process forever, but for now, I would recommend stopping after this second round of questions. Going through further rounds likely wouldn't earn you enough new insights to warrant the time spent. The only exception is if you feel there are major gaps left to explore—in that case, I'll leave it up to your best judgment. Either way, by this point you should have a much more fleshed out idea of the specifics of your story.

A Record of the Day

Finally, your last task for today is to write down everything you've discovered in a short, one to two paragraph summary. Much like the list you created yesterday, this summary will act as a brief record of your current ideas. Imagine a close friend asking you to describe the events of your story—what you write here is what you'd tell them in response.

So, below your questions and answers, write a summary that briefly explains the events of your story, any major twists or important backstory, and your various characters. Try to sum up everything you learned from the questions you answered today. We'll be returning to this summary later in the challenge as we further explore your premise.

By now, your draft outline <u>should</u> have:

- Your one to two sentence premise
- A short list covering the basics of your story
- **A one or two paragraph story summary**

By now, your draft outline <u>might</u> have:

- Notes about your original inspiration.
- A longer paragraph describing your full, high-concept idea

The Goals of Day Three

After such a thorough round of questioning, I hope you're feeling confident about the viability of your story. While brainstorming so many possibilities can feel exhausting, doing so proves that your idea has the potential to become a fully fledged novel. Instead of getting halfway through your draft only to realize your story isn't working, this process will help you move forward with confidence.

Not only that, but this series of intense questioning lets you know your story is reaching its full potential. It can be easy to write a novel based on whatever first comes to mind, however, our immediate instincts are often our most obvious ones:

- "I'm writing a medieval fantasy, so of course the knight in shining armor will be the good guy."
- "My story is about a suave, deadly spy, so they can't have a loving family waiting for them back home."
- "This is a romantic drama, so the guy has to get the girl by the end."
- "I'm writing literary fiction, so no way can there be space battles or all-powerful wizards."

No matter what genre you're writing in, there will always be common themes and conventions that storytellers have used a thousand times before. There's nothing innately bad about these, but many writers follow this well-trodden path with little thought. However, if we pause to observe our instincts more carefully, suddenly we see options we didn't know existed and our stories stand stronger as a result. There's nothing wrong with leaning into tropes, but the key is doing so knowingly—not blindly!

Ultimately, that was the purpose of today's goals. Not only did you expand on your ideas, but you challenged your first instincts. You looked closer at the variety of options hidden behind your premise and got to decide what *you* wanted your story to become.

Tomorrow we'll put these new ideas to work, but for now, here are the goals you've completed for Day Three:

1. Create a set of ten questions based on your premise.
2. Answer each of these questions with two separate answers, and then highlight the sections of your answers you like the most.
3. Rewrite your ten highlighted answers in their own list and create a new question for each of them.
4. Repeat the above process for these new questions.
5. Write a one to two paragraph story summary based on the new information you've learned.

On to Day Four!

4

DAY FOUR: THE START OF YOUR STORY'S SCENES

OVER THE PAST THREE DAYS, you've made some major decisions about the direction of your story. Fortunately, today is when all of that hard work will start to bear fruit, because today you'll begin creating the scenes that will ultimately form your novel!

Of course, I don't want to give you the wrong impression—this definitely won't be a breeze. There's a lot of creative work required at this stage of the challenge and, while it's rewarding, it's not easy.

Still, this is one of my favorite days of the journey. While I love the raw brainstorming that takes place during Days One, Two, and Three, there's just something immensely gratifying about seeing those possibilities take shape as an actual story. From here on out, you won't be working with only a vague framework of ideas. Instead, you'll trade that out for scenes and—by Day Seven—a fully functioning plot.

Today is the start of that transition.

Understanding the Basics of Scenes

As usual, you'll begin by pulling out your draft outline. Your goal for today is to create a list of twenty or more potential scenes for your story, and the story summary you created yesterday is the best place to start.

Of course, before you can begin this list, you'll need to know exactly what I mean when I say "scene."

In their simplest form, scenes are the individual events of your novel that come together to form your overall story. Often, people mistakenly think an individual scene equates to a single chapter and, while this may seem like a helpful way to understand scenes on the surface, it isn't always true. In fact, chapters are often built from one or two scenes that flow naturally together. So if a scene isn't the same thing as a chapter, then what is it?

Well, a scene is a section of your story defined by its own micro conflict. It's a continuous chain of actions by your cast as they move towards a *goal*, confront a *challenge, succeed or fail*, and then *react* to those events. Each scene in your novel will ultimately combine to lead your cast towards the end of your story and the final resolution of your conflict.

Even if you have a hard time understanding the definition of scenes, you can probably still identify one by feel. To help with this, it's easiest to think of them in the context of movies. In film a scene is very visual, and most scenes are separated by a change in location or time.

Think of Frodo agreeing to take the One Ring to Mordor in the first *Lord of the Rings* movie. This scene begins during the Council of Elrond where the various characters are arguing about who is fit to carry such a dangerous object. During this debate, Frodo feels the ring calling to him and agrees to take on the challenge. As a result, the Fellowship of the Ring is formed, and the scene ends.

There's a clear progression of events here:

- The Council must decide who will take the ring.
- No one can agree on someone fit to take it.
- Frodo volunteers and the Council decides they can trust him the most of everyone present.
- The group rallies behind Frodo and forms the Fellowship of the Ring.

Of course, this small conflict of deciding who will take the One Ring is just one of other micro conflicts that build into the main conflict of the entire *Lord of the Rings* trilogy— defeating the villain Sauron and destroying the One Ring.

So, based on this breakdown, think back to the premise I created in previous chapters. Here's what a scene in that story might look like:

- The main character, Varya, needs to contact her superiors back in the USSR.
- Her adoptive parents want to show her their town and end up taking her to a small town fair.
- Varya sneaks away to receive her next target, only to be found by her adoptive mother.
- Varya lies about who she was calling and her mother accepts the lie, much to Varya's relief.

While we'll be revisiting your scenes on Day Eight, this simple progression of a goal, challenge, outcome, and finally a reaction is the foundation of every scene you'll write. In fact, if you took the time you could create a breakdown like this for every scene in any novel or movie you choose!

Beginning Your List

With this basic explanation of scenes out of the way, you can return to your draft outline. Take a moment to read your story summary from yesterday, specifically thinking about your story's conflict. While there will inevitably be twists and turns along the way, every scene in your novel needs to move your cast closer to resolving this main conflict, so you'll want to keep it in mind as you complete today's goals.

To help you do that, skip a line or two in your outline and write this conflict down. Try your best to sum it up in a single sentence, to ensure you have a clear idea of what it is.

From there, you can begin brainstorming for your list of twenty scenes!

Depending on how much you know about your story, this process could go a few different ways. You may have a vivid idea of how your story ends, down to the final line your main character says, or you may only know that the final confrontation will take place in a snowy courtyard. Likewise, you may have a great idea for a magical scene where your characters explore a vast network of glowing, watery caves, or you may only know that you want them to explore an unknown location at some point.

At this stage, both of these answers are equally acceptable, and you should record them in your outline regardless of how much detail you can provide.

Unlike the example scenes we used to explain what scenes are, you don't need to worry about defining each element of your scenes just yet. Those were simply meant to help you understand the basic formation of scenes. On the other hand, this step is about getting the framework of your scenes down on paper.

For instance, in my own writing I'll often use just a single phrase or two to describe a scene at this early stage, later fleshing that phrase out as I get a better idea of how it'll fit within my larger story. You might know more details from the start, or you may be in the same boat—either way is perfectly fine.

To help jumpstart this process, your story summary from yesterday is the easiest place to start. By breaking it down into a beginning, middle, and ending you should be able to tease out at least three or four scenes right off the bat.

Consider these three questions:

- What scene begins your story?
- What scene ends it?
- What conflicts form the scenes in the middle of your story?

As you come up with scenes, write them down in a numbered list in your draft outline. Again, provide as much detail and information as you can, but don't worry if you only have a loose idea of how your scenes go—that's ok. For the bulk of your list, just try to cover what is taking place, who is involved, and why.

At the end of this process, your list should end up looking something like this:

- Varya showing off her skills as a KGB agent.
- Varya will need to receive her secret mission.

- A scene when Varya meets her new parents on the tarmac after arriving in the United States.
- Varya is brought along to the town fair, and spends the whole scene struggling to sneak away and contact her superiors, only to be caught by her adoptive mother.
- Varya gets lost in the snow.
- Varya is caught by her adoptive parents with a letter that outlines the final phase of her mission. They finally find out why she is really there.
- After they learn the truth, Varya will need to convince her family she is actually on their side, but she'll fail at first.
- A group meeting with the head of the KGB, Kostya.

Notice how some of these scenes are fully formed ideas, while others are simply requirements. I know that, at some point, my main character will have to arrive and meet her new family. I also know that she'll need to regain their trust when they find out who she really is. Alongside these requirements, I also have scenes that are just basic ideas I hope to incorporate, such as "Varya gets lost in the snow."

Once you've written down as many scenes as you can glean from your story summary—along with any you already had in mind—you'll want to shift focus to your story's requirements. Again, you may have already covered some of these requirements in your current list, but it's likely you still have a few you'll need to fulfill.

Here are some scenes your story will need:

- A scene that introduces your main character.
- A scene that introduces your villain.

- At least one scene that introduces any sidekicks, allies, enemies, or mentors of your main character.
- At least one scene that introduces the world your story takes place in, its society, and any rules or worldbuilding your readers will need to know.
- A scene that introduces the conflict of your story.
- At least one scene where your main character gets involved with the conflict or "sets out on their journey," so to speak.
- A variety of scenes that test and challenge your main character as they work towards their goals.
- At least one scene where your main character challenges or is challenged by your villain.
- At least one scene that shows the final culmination of your story's conflict, along with your main character's role in that culmination.
- At least one scene that shows what your story's world will look like once the conflict is over.

Some of the scenes you create might fulfill multiple of these requirements, while others will only serve one purpose. Both of these situations are fine, however, you'll want to ensure that you cover all of these requirements in some way.

Of course, as you continue creating your list, don't worry about writing your scenes in any particular order. You may find that some scenes logically connect to one another—and I encourage you to mark them as a set if they do—but most of the scenes you create today will be standalone. You'll be sorting through them and figuring out how they fit into your larger story later on.

You also shouldn't worry if you end up creating over twenty scenes. Today, your focus should just be on identifying as many scenes as you can, aiming for *at least* twenty.

Creating a Foundation

Now, all of this raises the question—why twenty scenes?

Well, twenty is somewhat of a middle ground, a compromise so to speak. While creating this book, I tested this process by writing a series of three different novels, and what I found was that twenty scenes was low enough to feel attainable at this early stage. However, it was also high enough that I could later expand on this list and still have a fully fleshed out story by the end.

You see, by the time your outline is complete, you should end up with between thirty and forty scenes—potentially even more.

While every genre has its own average length, most novels comfortably land somewhere between sixty thousand and eighty thousand words. Of course, some novels, especially fantasy and science fiction, are much longer. On the other hand, many recent novels come in at only fifty thousand words thanks to the influence of National Novel Writing Month, since fifty thousand is the target word count for that challenge. Either way, when you consider that the average scene is about two thousand words, you can make an easy calculation.

75,000 (avg. words in a novel)/2,000 (avg. words in a scene) = 38 (avg. scenes needed)

In practice this won't be quite so simple, because while the average length of a scene is two thousand words, not every scene will be that long. However, this simple bit of math does allow you to set rough goals for your own story.

By aiming for twenty scenes now, you have about half of the

scenes you'll need going forward. This is the skeleton of your story, and as the challenge progresses you'll start to develop more of the connective tissue that will bind these twenty scenes together.

By the end, you should be able to sit comfortably within that thirty to forty scene threshold, simply by building off of the foundation you created today.

A Beginning, Middle, and End

At this point, you should have a long list of twenty or more scenes, but this list is only so helpful in its current form. Your scenes are likely in no particular order, and it'll be hard to see how they flow into a cohesive story when they're so disorganized. Thus, your next task is to sort these scenes into groups based on their chronology.

To do this, copy each scene into the group it best fits under:

- **Beginning:** This is where you introduce your readers to your novel's world and characters, as well as establish the start of your story's conflict.
- **Middle:** Here your main character and the rest of your cast will struggle to resolve your story's conflict in their favor. In the process they'll face various tests, trials, victories, and setbacks, forming the bulk of your story.
- **End:** This is the run up and final culmination of your conflict, along with a few scenes showing the aftermath of this confrontation and the effects its outcome will have on your story's world.

This should be fairly straightforward for most scenes, but there will inevitably be a few that don't quite fit anywhere.

These will likely be the scenes you could only describe with a handful of words, or that you didn't know how to work into your larger story. For now, don't worry about them. Simply leave them in their own group labeled "Undecided".

Additionally, the scenes in your three groups—just like in your previous list—don't need to be in any particular order within each group. In fact, they may still only be loosely connected. That's ok, because your outline will stay flexible for a few more days. So long as these scenes chronologically fit under the same label, you'll be just fine as we continue into tomorrow.

Finally, as you've gone through this process you've hopefully developed a better idea of how these three parts of your story will progress. Now is the time to make a record of those ideas.

Write a brief paragraph at the top of each group that explains what happens throughout that group's scenes. These don't need to be very long, only four or five sentences in total. Do one for each section—beginning, middle, and end—based on the scenes you grouped together and on the story summary you created yesterday. These will make a big difference as you expand on your scenes tomorrow, giving you a rough framework in which to place new scenes and reorganize old ones.

Sketching Out Your World

Finally, we've reached the last of today's goals.

While creating your list of possible scenes, I imagine you developed a pretty solid idea of the rules of your story's world. You'll need to reference those worldbuilding rules tomorrow, making today the best time to write down a brief paragraph explaining your story's time period, technology, environment, social norms, and cultures. Depending on the story you're writing, you may also want to explain any events running concurrent to your story, such as wars or scientific advancements.

> **A Quick Note:** If you're writing anything referencing real world history, I encourage you to take an hour or two to research critical facts about your chosen time period or event. There's no need to go overboard—in fact, please limit yourself so you don't spend weeks on this task—but understanding the facts now will save you from a lot of painful rewrites later on.

Taking this time to think about worldbuilding is especially important for fantasy and science fiction novels, which may have complex magic or scientific systems that aren't present in our real world. However, even if your story is firmly grounded in reality, you should still take the time to complete this step.

By writing down these basic facts about your story's time period, social norms, and technologies, you'll be able to avoid common but embarrassing mistakes, like writing about a character using a cell phone in your 1950s London spy thriller!

By now, your draft outline should have:

- Your one to two sentence premise
- A short list covering the basics of your story
- A one or two paragraph story summary
- **A list of 20+ potential scenes separated into beginning, middle, and end with brief paragraphs describing each group**

- **A paragraph covering basic rules and facts about your story's world**

By now, your draft outline <u>might</u> have:

- Notes about your original inspiration
- A longer paragraph describing your full, high-concept idea
- **A small group of "Undecided" scenes**

The Goals of Day Four

As I said earlier on, <u>the scenes you created today will be the foundation of your outline going forward</u>. However, that doesn't mean everything has come together just yet.

If you're still unsure how your final story will turn out, don't worry. You'll be expanding on these scenes a lot in the coming days, shuffling them around until the pieces slot together in a way you're happy with. This will involve a few more important elements that we haven't explored yet, so it's natural to feel uncertain at this stage.

Still, I hope you're excited about the state your outline is in. You have the start of actual scenes within your grasp, and these will eventually become the words, paragraphs, and chapters you'll read when you hold your finished novel in your hands. Your story is starting to take shape!

Tomorrow we'll start to form a cohesive storyline, but for now, here are the goals you've completed for Day Four:

- Brainstorm a list of 20+ potential scenes that fulfill the various requirements of your story.

- Divide these 20+ scenes into three groups—beginning, middle, and end.
- Write a brief paragraph for each group describing what happens in that section of your story.
- Create a short paragraph going over the rules of your story's world and any important elements of worldbuilding you'll need to know later.

On to Day Five!

5

DAY FIVE: FORMING A SCENE TIMELINE

MOST OF US have at least one TV show or series we like to indulge in, but you may feel bad for giving in to these guilty pleasures—especially when you have more important work demanding your attention. However, I have some good news! Today you'll get a free pass to binge watch as much as you want, so long as you get some busywork out of the way in the process.

You see, today's goals require a lot of tedious, organizational work. Day Five is all about building your story's timeline and sorting through the scenes you created yesterday, and while this is an important part of the process, it can get extremely monotonous.

This is why having something else to focus on will be so helpful today. Instead of putting all of your mental energy towards a single, repetitive task, you can enjoy a show while still accomplishing today's goals. When you're feeling particularly stuck, just tune out your outline for a few minutes, relax with your chosen media, and return to working a bit more refreshed.

So, instead of beginning today by pulling out your draft outline, pick a movie or TV show you enjoy—but won't find *too* distracting—grab something to drink, and find a stack of index cards. It's time to connect the scenes of your story!

Preparing Your Index Cards

I can already imagine some of your questions: "Index cards? Why can't I just use my draft outline?"

Well, while your draft outline is a great tool, today you'll need to begin branching out. A stack of large index cards and some colored pens will go a long way towards making the next few days of this challenge easier—especially as we continue tweaking the events of your story. By writing your scenes out on individuals cards, you'll find repositioning and reorganizing them far more intuitive in the long run.

For today's goals, you'll also want to find a large, flat, and preferably undisturbed surface to work on. Personally, I tend to lay my index cards out on the floor, but a kitchen table or even a counter would work just as well. So long as you have enough space to spread out and move scenes around, you should be good to go!

From there, your first goal for today is a simple one—create one index card for each of the twenty scenes in the list you created yesterday.

This is where you'll want to flip on your choice of show, pull out some fancy pens, and grab a stack of index cards. While this is by far the most tedious aspect of today's work, bear with me, because the benefits will become clear before the day is over.

Your index cards should follow a simple format:

On the lined side:

- Describe the scene in a word or two.
- Explain the setting where the scene takes place.
- List who is in the scene.
- Briefly describe what's happening.
- Provide a short explanation for why this is happening.

On the blank side:

- The descriptive phrase you wrote above.
- Leave the rest blank for later work.

Here's an example index card based on one of the scenes I created yesterday:

On the lined side:

- The Town Fair
- A stereotypical American summer fair filled with junk food, straw bales, and rides. It's on the edge of town at dusk, and the neon lights are a focus.
- Varya, her adoptive parents and siblings, the town's pastor, a girl her age who she'll soon be going to school with, and two of the highschool's football players.
- Varya is brought along to a fair soon after arriving at

her new home. She spends the whole scene struggling to sneak away and contact her superiors amid the crowded streets. At the end, she's caught by her adoptive mother.

- Varya needs to receive her next assignment, and she doesn't want to check in late and disappoint her superiors. She desperately wants to prove herself, so failure isn't an option.

On the blank side:

- The Town Fair
- (blank)

———

As was the case when creating your list of scenes yesterday, don't worry about writing your answers in tons of detail, or even about skipping some if you have to. Today is simply about laying the groundwork for later days in the challenge.

By Day Nine, each scene in your story should have all of these blanks filled in—and potentially a few more, though we'll get to that later on. For now, simply fill in as much as you can and move on to the next card.

Of course, some of the more in-depth scenes you create may not fit neatly on a standard index card. In that case, feel free to write your ideas in shorthand while still covering who is in the scene, what's happening, and why.

Once you have all twenty or more index cards complete, you can move on to organizing them in a timeline.

This timeline will be similar to the groups you created yesterday, so you can use those as a starting point. However, to create your timeline we'll be going a step beyond those groups and sorting your scenes chronologically. Simply lay your index cards out so that each scene is in order, with the one that occurs prior above and the one after below.

While this may seem simple on the surface, this is probably where you'll spend the bulk of your time today, so here are some steps to make the process easier:

1. Using the groups you created yesterday for reference, first lay down any scenes that you know occur at a certain point in your story. These will be your framing scenes.
2. For scenes that are part of a set, keep them clustered together in your lineup.
3. Once you have all of your framing scenes placed, spread them out to make space between them— again, keeping sets together.
4. Begin loosely placing the rest of your scenes between these framing scenes, stacking them together to sort in a moment.
5. Once all of your scenes are placed somewhere within your timeline, pick up one stack at a time and sort them chronologically until you have a logical order for that section.
6. Move on to complete this for every stack you created until all of them are organized between your framing scenes.

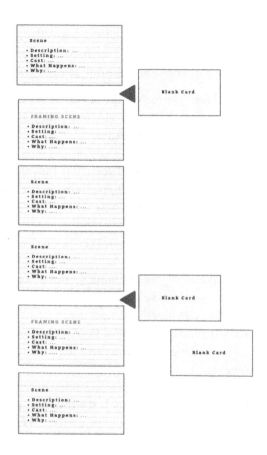

During this process, you'll likely discover holes in your timeline where new scenes should go. In those instances, simply add a blank placeholder card—or multiple, if you think that section needs a lot more fleshing out. Of course, if you get ideas for new scenes while doing this, quickly make a new index card and slot it into place!

You may also find that you're unsure exactly where some

index cards should go. For now, that's ok. Simply place them as close as you can within your timeline, setting them just to the side of your current lineup to make it clear their placement is still uncertain. You may also want to mark them lightly with a pencil, in case they get shuffled around later on.

For any scenes you have no idea how to incorporate, set them aside in a dedicated pile.

Expanding Your Timeline

This is when you might want to switch off the show you've been listening to so far, because we're about to get into more analytical territory.

With your timeline created, you should be able to see at a glance where the biggest holes are in your current story. Anywhere you have large groups of blank index cards will be a logical place to expand. However, there are some other important questions you'll also need to consider:

- How does your story begin?
- How does it end?
- What begins your story's conflict?
- How does your main character learn of this conflict?
- When does your main character get involved?
- When does your cast meet?
- When does your main character meet your villain?
- When does your villain start playing an active role in your story?
- How does your story challenge and test your main character?
- What will your main character need to do to succeed

against the villain or, alternatively, what do they fail to do that causes them to lose?

After considering the questions above, scan through your timeline. Do the scenes you currently have cover all of these elements? If not, which questions are left unanswered, and what would you need to do to fix that?

The reason this is so important is because the questions above are all critical components of your final story, meaning it's well worth taking the time to ensure they're answered at this point in your outline. You'll likely find that you can add information to existing scenes to address many of these, while other questions will benefit from a scene all their own, potentially replacing one of the blank index cards you had in your timeline previously.

From there, once you've answered this initial set of questions in your timeline, you can address other questions more specific to *your* story.

For instance, are there any points where groups of your characters suddenly know each other, without a scene that shows them meet? Do any of your characters have strong relationships form mid-story, and are those relationships developed in a believable way? Have your characters gained any skills or knowledge without going through the process of learning first?

Take your time to brainstorm as many questions as you can and explore any of the missing pieces of your current story. What you're ultimately trying to do here is expand your timeline by adding or tweaking scenes to ensure your story flows in a logical, cohesive way.

Ideally, this process will result in you filling in most of your blank index cards, even if you only have a short phrase or idea to add to them. Aim to leave only around five or six cards blank after this process is complete. Remember, it's ok if you haven't fully fleshed out each element yet—your goal is just to start as many scenes as possible with as much information as you can provide.

By the end of this, you'll want to have expanded your timeline to include at least thirty scenes, if not more (including your blank index cards).

How Everything Fits Together

With your timeline now organized and expanded, you've completed the bulk of your work for today. However, you may be wondering how these index cards will ultimately fit into your outline. Before today is over, should you take the time to write these scenes in your draft outline?

The short answer is—no.

Your timeline will continue to grow a lot over the next few days, and you don't want to spend a large amount of time recording it in your draft outline only to change it tomorrow. At the end of this process, you'll get to neatly record your final timeline in your Master Outline, but for now, keeping it on index cards is your best option.

Of course, you should still keep track of your timeline's current state. In my opinion, the easiest way to do this is by snapping a quick photo, but you're also welcome to number each scene lightly with a pencil. Just make sure it'll be easy to erase if that scene's position changes later on.

Once you've done this, stack up your index cards—keeping

them in chronological order for tomorrow—and wrap them with a rubber band or a binder clip.

By now, your draft outline <u>should</u> have:

- Your one to two sentence premise
- A short list covering the basics of your story
- A one or two paragraph story summary
- A list of 20+ potential scenes separated into beginning, middle, and end with brief paragraphs describing each group
- A paragraph covering basic rules and facts about your story's world
- **A scene timeline (kept separate from your draft outline)**

By now, your draft outline <u>might</u> have:

- Notes about your original inspiration
- A longer paragraph describing your full, high-concept idea
- A small group of "Undecided" scenes
- **A photo of your Day Five timeline**

The Goals of Day Five

Today has been all about <u>getting your story not only organized, but coherent</u>. Whereas yesterday was focused on creating the puzzle pieces, today you began fitting them together into something resembling a completed picture. Of course, there are still holes, with the most glaring one being a lack of fleshed out characters.

Fortunately, that'll be your task for tomorrow, so you won't have to wait much longer!

However, before we wrap up for today, I have a quick aside. You see, probably the most gratifying part of today's work is that you now have something of a finished story on your hands—and because of this, many writers stop at this stage, knowingly or not. Some feel that, once they have the loose framework of a story in place, they can and will dive into their first draft and figure out the rest as they go.

Yet, as I'm sure you've noticed, we're only halfway through this challenge. This is because your current story is lacking well-defined characters, along with a few critical structural elements. It's easy to overlook these pieces of your story, but the consequences of doing so can deeply affect your writing.

By outlining these parts of your story upfront, you save yourself the time spent writing tens of thousands of words "figuring it out." This way, when you sit down to begin your first draft, you'll know exactly where you're going and won't have to struggle through the kind of writer's block that can cripple an early novel. Plus, you won't have to sacrifice the exciting feeling of exploring your story's potential either— you'll simply experience that feeling through your outline, instead of your first draft. Likewise, when it's time to edit your manuscript into a finished novel, you're much less likely to face major rewrites. You've dealt with the difficult questions upfront, and the payoff is a much smoother writing experience from start to finish.

Either way, whether you've been the type who figures it out as you go in the past or you've always been an avid outliner, stick with me. There are only five days left in the challenge, and you're officially halfway there!

Tomorrow we'll finally flesh out your story's cast, but for now, here are the goals you've completed for Day Five:

1. Create index cards for each of your 20+ scenes.
2. Spread these index cards out on a large, flat surface and organize them in chronological order, adding blank index cards wherever you feel your story could be expanded upon.
3. Using a series of questions, fill out this timeline until you have 30+ scenes, leaving as few blank cards as possible.
4. Take a photo or otherwise mark the index cards in your timeline to reference later in the challenge.

On to Day Six!

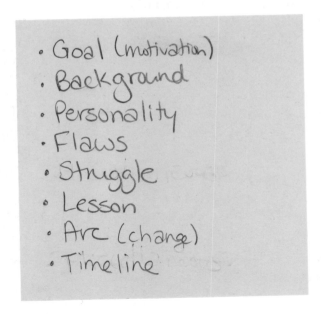

- Goal (motivation)
- Background
- Personality
- Flaws
- Struggle
- Lesson
- Arc (change)
- Timeline

6

DAY SIX: CREATING THE CHARACTER SHEET

WITH HALF of this challenge behind us, today is the day we'll finally begin turning our attention to the craft behind fiction writing—starting with your characters.

Of course, since characters are such a critical part of your final novel, it's reasonable to wonder why we've waited until Day Six to explore your story's cast. After all, as you've established your premise and timeline, you've undoubtedly begun to develop ideas for the characters that will ultimately populate your story. However, if we had moved today's goals to an earlier point in the challenge, you'd have likely found yourself unable to finish most of them.

Characters are one of the hardest aspects of storytelling, because a well-written character should come alive on the page. Throughout your novel they'll grow and evolve into unique, expressive people, but first you have to create a world for them to live in. That's why you established the basics of your story first—these form the foundation you need to understand your characters' goals and motivations as we move forward.

This is also why we aren't diving into story structure and your story's plot until tomorrow. Just like you need a rough idea of your story to explore your characters, you'll be using those same characters to create your plot over the next two days.

So, don't worry! By the end of the challenge, you'll have a cohesive story where your characters and plot are intertwined in ways both memorable and impactful for your readers—but first, you'll need to bring your cast to life!

Sorting Out Who's Who

Until now, I've been using generic terms like "main character" and "villain" to describe the various members of your story's cast. This was done to make it easier for people to understand, because not everyone reading this will have experience with the different terms used to describe characters. Generic terms were necessary, even if they weren't ideal.

However, today is where we'll finally start using some more technical language, because by now you should be getting more comfortable with the many elements of storytelling. From now on, I'll describe your story's main character using the actual term—protagonist. Likewise, I'll refer to your villain as your antagonist.

This is for a few reasons, but most importantly, it's about clarity. For starters, these terms are more specific. As you learn more about the craft of storytelling, you'll start to realize that not every main character is the protagonist, and not every antagonist is a traditional villain. Using these more clearly defined terms is important, because I'm sure at least one of you has been wondering over the past few days, "But my main character's opponent isn't an evil villain!"

Today I'm going to set the record straight and prepare you for this slight shift in terminology. Here are the terms you'll need to know going forward:

————

Protagonist:

This is the traditional "hero" of your story, and will usually be your main character. Your protagonist is the agent of change within your plot and has the largest role in resolving your conflict. They are also who your audience will identify with the most.

- **Examples:** Luke Skywalker, Bilbo Baggins, Tony Stark, Aang, Dorothy Gale, Katniss Everdeen, Anakin Skywalker, Princess Nausicaä

Antagonist:

This character is the main opponent of your protagonist, and their job is to block your protagonist from achieving their goals. Your antagonist will likely be another character that lives in your story's world, but they could also be anything from a raging dragon to a great white whale, or even part of your protagonist's own mind.

However, they can also be more subtle and less outright evil. Many antagonists are just characters whose goals oppose the protagonist's, even if those goals aren't of the "evil villain" variety.

Ultimately, the best antagonists act as a mirror of your protagonist's worst traits—a protagonist who struggles with anger will learn the most by fighting against an antagonist whose vice is rage.

- **Examples:** Darth Vader, Smaug, The Wicked Witch of the West, Mr. Wickham, Ursula, Princess Kushana, King Claudius, Loki

Allies:

All stories—even the most isolating ones—will support their protagonists with allies of some kind. These characters might provide advice, physical aid, moral support, or even just friendship, but they can also betray your protagonist if the relationship goes sour.

- **Examples:** Dr. John Watson, Samwise Gamgee, Chewbacca, Jarvis, The Tin Man, Mushu, Timon and Pumba, 007's Quartermaster

Mentors:

While you may think of wiry old wizards when you imagine a mentor, mentors can actually come in many forms. Their role is to provide moral, spiritual, and plot related guidance to your cast throughout their journey. In mythology, the advice and gifts mentors give are almost always the key the protagonist will need to overcome the myth's conflict.

- **Examples:** Gandalf, Obi-wan Kenobi, General Iroh, Grandmother Willow, Professor Charles Xavier, Mary Poppins, Mr. Miyagi, Lionel Logue

---

Some members of your cast may only serve one of these roles—particularly your protagonist—but others can exist in a grey area. For instance, Lionel Logue is definitely a mentor to Prince Albert in *The King's Speech*, but he also becomes an ally by the end of the movie.

Ultimately, these terms are important to know, both for this challenge, but also for your future storytelling endeavors. When someone asks about your protagonist's mentor or about the ally-turned-antagonist that you worked so hard to create, you want to be equipped to answer them. After all, your novel will likely have many nuances and quirks, and having the right terms to describe those unique elements will be a critical skill when you start sharing your story with the world!

Starting Your List

Before we can make any progress fleshing out your cast, you'll first need to have that cast written down. This will be a big help when it comes to keeping everyone organized. Fortunately, you've probably come up with a lot of ideas for characters over the past few days, so you should have a solid idea of who will populate your story's world.

To start this process, simply pull out your draft outline and write a list of every character that plays a repeated role in your story. This doesn't need to include utility characters, specifically ones that are only there to perform a single task, such as the pilot who flies your character from point A to B or the grocery clerk that bags their food while they're busy checking their phone.

If you already have names for these characters, that's great—

feel free to use those in your list. However, even if you don't, that's ok too! We'll be naming everyone in a moment, so for now, simply write a clear description of who they are and what role they'll play. Be thorough here, making sure to include every character you can think of that plays an active role in your story.

Once you have your list created, we can get to the fun part!

First up, you'll need to alphabetize this list—but of course, that requires names. Any characters you've already named will be easy, but for those you haven't, take a moment to consider what kind of name would suit them. Any of the online baby naming databases are a great resource for doing this, so I recommend starting your search there. Most of them let you filter for names with specific meanings, origins, languages, and genders. Your chosen names may change later on—they won't be set in stone until you've published your novel, after all—but it's helpful to have a name you feel fits the character you're talking about.

As you go, write down these newly named characters, organizing your list until you've named every character and put them in alphabetical order.

Of course, while going through this process you may start to wonder why we're bothering to alphabetize this list at all, and I can tell you this—it's not just for your own ease of use. In fact, this list is actually more for your readers than for you. You see, readers will probably need a few scenes or even whole chapters before they can clearly remember your characters' names. In the intervening time it's easy to get them confused, and this is doubly true when their names start with similar letters.

Every author has a set of letters they lean towards when naming characters, and by alphabetizing your list you can figure out what yours are. Personally, I tend to use a lot of "Sa" names:

- Samuel,
- Saria,
- Sable,
- Saxon, et cetera...

On the other hand, J.R.R. Tolkien seems to love "V" names:

- Vairë,
- Varda,
- Vëantur,
- Valandil, et cetera...

If you saw those four characters early in a story, how likely would you be able to remember who they were, even a few pages later? Not very.

> (And yes, all four of those Tolkien characters came from the *Silmarillion*, if you were wondering.)

To help prevent this confusion, I encourage you to go back through your alphabetized list and rename any characters whose names are too similar. You can even go so far as to cover every letter of the alphabet before your let yourself repeat any beginning letters. While naming conventions can be great, such as triplets being named Harry, Harriet, and Harvey, you should always do this purposefully, never on accident.

Think of it this way—you may discover a new name you wouldn't have used otherwise, falling in love with it *and* the character it's attached to in the process!

The Character Sheet

With the list you've created now in hand, we're getting closer to starting your character sheet.

By the end of today this sheet will be comprised of two parts, meant to organize and explain every member of your cast. The main part will simply be the character sheet itself. Any character that is significant enough to be named or that will play a repeated role in your story will be recorded here. Alongside this sheet, your protagonist and a few other core characters will get their own, more detailed pages.

However, before creating this character sheet, we have one more task to complete—labeling your core cast.

This core cast will obviously include your protagonist and antagonist, but it'll also include important mentor figures, allies, and enemies. Essentially, these are the most active players in your story. To pick out these characters, you'll need to consider what role they'll play in your final novel:

- Do they have a significant influence on the outcome of your conflict?
- Will they be a regular presence throughout your protagonist's journey?
- Do they oppose or challenge your protagonist and/or their allies in a meaningful way?
- Will readers see them grow or change significantly as the story progresses?

- Do they meaningfully impact your protagonist, either as an ally, mentor, or enemy?

Any character that fulfills one or more of the requirements above will probably earn a place within your core cast, so mark their names in your list. By the time you've finished testing your characters against these questions, your core cast should end up being anywhere from five to ten characters. However, depending on the type of story you're writing, your core cast may be much larger. A sprawling fantasy epic will naturally have a more expansive cast than a short, cozy romance novel.

Of course, while this group of core characters will ultimately play the biggest role in your story, that doesn't mean the characters you leave out are any less important. These other characters add color, texture, and life to your story's world, and will all influence the direction of your protagonist's journey in their own ways. The main benefit of labeling your core cast at this stage is simply one of convenience.

These are the characters you'll be dealing with the most, both throughout the rest of this challenge and while writing your novel. While they'll be getting mostly the same treatment as the other characters in your character sheet, making them easy to identify now will save you a lot of time later on. Personally, I even like to highlight the names of my core cast members so I can easily reference them at a glance—how you mark yours is up to you.

With all of this setup complete, you can finally create your character sheet. This sheet will follow a simple structure:

Character's Name:

Write a short description of who this character is, what role they play in your story, and what relationships they might have with other characters.

- Your character's main goal
- A brief paragraph outlining their background or personal history
- Key terms to describe their personality
- Additional terms to describe their flaws
- Any other important information you want to record, such as physical appearance, skills, or special knowledge

———

Once you've done this for one character, repeat this process for your entire cast—it's really that simple.

Every character in your story, even if they aren't a core character, will have a goal of some kind. This can be something simple like wanting to win a contest or learn to ride a bike, or it could be more complex, like struggling to live up to the expectations of a beloved teacher. Likewise, every character will have a history. There's no need to go into tons of depth here, but try to write a short paragraph that gives you a basic idea of where they've come from and what their life has been like so far.

Last on the list, you'll want to describe their personality. This will largely be influenced by their background and the kind of role you want them to play. A begrudging tutor may be lazy but secretly passionate about an obscure topic they fell in love with during college, while the beloved local gardener might be comedic and quick-witted under their harsh, sunburnt face. Whatever their personality is, try to describe it using a few, strong words.

Not, let's think back to our example protagonist, which I've named Varya. This is what her entry might look like:

———

Varya:

The protagonist, a Soviet teen sent to spy on a family of US special operatives with access to important state secrets, she is the prodigy of the head of the Soviet KGB.

- **Goal:** Varya wants to rise in the ranks of the KGB and gain respect from her superiors.
- **Background:** Varya wasn't born a native Russian. She's actually from Georgia, a Soviet republic. As she got older, she was taught to idolize Russia. When her classmates protested Soviet control, she ratted them out, resulting in them being killed and her being rewarded with a job in the Soviet KGB as an operative. She's slowly risen in the ranks since that incident.
- **Personality:** Driven, determined, intelligent
- **Flaws:** Bottled-up, aggressive, quick to judge others
- **Miscellaneous:** She borders on scrawny in appearance, but she's physically strong despite this. She's particularly proud of her ability to speak many languages.

———

You'll be relying on your character sheet a lot in the coming days, so don't skimp here—especially for your core cast. Feel free to go into as much detail as you need, even if you're unsure whether that information will end up in your final novel.

The real value of this sheet is that it gives you a strong idea of who your characters are as people. When you sit down to write, understanding your characters' upbringing and fears will help you write them in a more realistic way. After all, we all react to our current lives and situations based on the beliefs, prejudices, and experiences of our pasts. In many ways, this personal history defines us as people, and the same should be true of your novel's cast.

Finally, as you create this sheet, make sure to keep your characters in alphabetical order—this time because it really is just easier for you to reference later on!

Questions to Ask Your Protagonist

By the time you've filled out your entire character sheet, you'll have created an in-depth reference covering all of your cast members, including your protagonist. However, because of the unique role your protagonist will play in your story, we're going to create a more detailed character profile, just for them.

This is because your protagonist is the main agent of change in your story and will have the biggest stake in your story's conflict. They'll be your focal point and the character most affected by your plot, so you'll naturally want to have a deeper understanding of their motivations, personality, background, and desires.

To start this, write your protagonist's name and transfer any information about them from your character sheet onto a separate page of your draft outline. Then, answer the twelve questions below:

- What is your protagonist's deepest flaw or internal struggle? How does this affect their everyday life?
- What difficult lesson or truth will they need to learn in order to grow or improve as a person?
- Will they succeed in learning this lesson?
- What is their primary goal in your story? How does this relate to their flaw?
- How does your protagonist think and behave?
- What do they believe about themselves and others?
- What is their best quality? What are they good at?
- What is their worst quality? What do they struggle with, and are they aware of this weakness?
- What do they want to do/achieve/change/see in their lifetime? How does this affect their decisions?
- How do they change as your story goes on? What prompts this change, and is it for the better?
- What are they most afraid of when the story begins? What are they most afraid of by the end?
- What is the most significant moment of their life prior to the beginning of your story?

Of course, some of these may not make sense at first glance, especially if you're not well-versed in the world of character creation. To help, here are some examples that should give you a better idea of how you could answer these questions for your own protagonist. All of these examples are written in the same order as the questions above:

- They based their value on the opinions of others, causing them to doubt their own self-worth.
- They don't need to conform to be loved.

- Yes, they will learn this lesson by the end!
- They want to gain their father's acceptance.
- They're clever and inventive, but very awkward.
- They believe they're weak and useless.
- They're an amazing builder and inventor.
- They're clumsy and difficult to talk to, and they're intensely aware of these flaws.
- Their greatest goal is to make their father proud, as a way of earning their place in their society.
- Not only do they value their own ideas and skills more and more, but they begin to realize that the ideals they had been striving towards weren't the best to begin with. This change begins in earnest after they meet a new and unusual friend.
- At the start, they're deeply afraid of being unwanted and alone. By the end, they're afraid of not only losing their new best friend, but of failing to protect their family as well.
- As a baby, they were attacked by dragons. This not only informs their own uneasiness towards dragons, but feeds their father's intense hatred of them as well.

Once you finish looking through these twelve questions and answering them like I did above, you should have a much better understanding of your protagonist as a person. Now, you simply need to apply this new knowledge to your protagonist's character profile, using the following template:

———

Protagonist's Name:

Write a short description of who your protagonist is, what

role they play in your story, and what relationships they might have with other characters.

- Your protagonist's main goal
- A short paragraph outlining their background or personal history
- Key terms to describe their personality
- Additional terms to describe their flaws
- The inner struggle they'll face
- The important lesson they'll need to learn
- Whether they succeed in learning that lesson
- Any other important information you want to record, such as physical appearance, skills, or special knowledge (you could even add a photo!)

————

This isn't drastically different from the rest of your character sheet, but it does include a few important additions unique to your protagonist. For instance, it has a much bigger focus on their internal struggles and on whether or not they grow and change as a character throughout your story—and whether that change is for the better.

Based on this template, let's take Varya's character sheet from earlier and expand on it, the same way you will for your own protagonist.

Here's what it looks like:

————

Varya:

The protagonist, a Soviet teen sent to spy on a family of US special operatives with access to important state secrets, she is the prodigy of the head of the Soviet KGB.

- **Goal:** Varya wants to rise in the ranks of the KGB and gain respect from her superiors.
- **Background:** Varya wasn't born a native Russian. She's actually from Georgia, a Soviet republic. As she got older, she was taught to idolize Russia. When her classmates protested Soviet control, she ratted them out, resulting in them being killed and her being rewarded with a job in the Soviet KGB as an operative. She's slowly risen in the ranks since that incident.
- **Personality:** Driven, determined, intelligent
- **Flaws:** Bottled-up, aggressive, quick to judge others
- **Struggle:** She believes people aren't worthy of respect unless they're useful
- **Lesson:** Everyone is worthwhile for their own unique reasons, herself included
- **Arc:** Yes - Positive Arc
- **Miscellaneous:** She borders on scrawny in appearance, but she's physically strong despite this. She's particularly proud of her ability to speak many languages.

———

As you can see, this adds a new layer to your character sheet. This will be important later on, specifically when you begin considering your protagonist's character arc.

Understanding Character Arcs

If you're wondering, I wasn't making the previous section's example up off the top of my head. Those are all based on Hiccup, the protagonist of *How to Train Your Dragon*. The mention of a "positive arc" in Varya's character profile was purposeful as well. You see, what you're ultimately doing with your protagonist's character profile is forming the skeleton of their character arc.

If you're not already familiar with these, a character arc is simply the inner journey your character goes on throughout your story. Character arcs are all about change, and they follow your character as they face their deepest inner flaw, hopefully learning an important lesson that will help them overcome that flaw along the way.

Within this basic framework, your character can go down one of three paths:

———

The Positive Arc:

This is the classic "hero" story, though it can apply equally to many types of characters.

In a positive arc the character starts out with a deep internal flaw. Throughout the course of their arc the story's conflict punishes this flaw. They face a major challenge that leads to a turning point in their arc, moving them closer to uncovering the lesson they need to learn. Ultimately—despite setbacks along the way—they learn to embrace this new truth, overcome their flaws, and succeed against the conflict of their story.

- **Examples:** Rick Blaine, Harry Potter, Aragorn, Han Solo, Hiccup

The Negative Arc:

Negative arcs follow a similar trajectory as positive arcs, with a major change at the end.

Just like a positive arc, the character begins the story with an internal flaw and—as the story progresses—uncovers an important truth, experiencing a key turning point along the way. However, unlike a positive arc, a negative arc character rejects that truth repeatedly. By the end of the story they're more entrenched in their flaws than before, growing into a worse version of themselves and failing to resolve the conflict of their story as a result.

- **Examples:** Anakin Skywalker, Jay Gatsby, Michael Corleone, Tyler Durden, Sansa Stark

The Flat Arc:

These are the black sheep of character arcs. While positive and negative arcs are "change arcs," a flat arc character already knows their truth (or lesson) at the start of the story. Instead, their arc is about upholding that truth in the face of their story's conflict, passing their lesson to others in the process.

- **Examples:** Captain America, Katniss Everdeen, Luke Skywalker, Princess Nausicaä, Mattie Ross

———

No matter what arc your character follows, you can see that

each of these has a similar structure—with flat arcs as the exception. Your character starts out deeply flawed in a way detrimental to their happiness and to the happiness of those around them. Through a series of tests and trials, they're asked to confront this flaw and embrace an important truth. They face a turning point where they seem to have solved their problems, before suffering a final major setback.

How they handle this setback will ultimately determine if they succeed or fail against their story's conflict. Of course, their success or failure also depends on whether or not they learn their lesson—which likewise depends on the type of character they are.

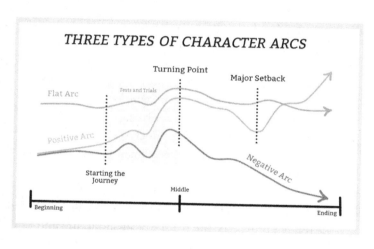

THREE TYPES OF CHARACTER ARCS

As you can see above, positive arc characters follow a mostly upward trend—with some setbacks—before eventually learning their truth and overcoming their flaw. Negative arc characters start out the same, but instead give in to their flaw and meet their downfall. Finally, flat arc characters already understand their truth at the start of their story, and must instead <u>struggle to prove that truth to others who are fighting against it.</u>

Since we've already been picking on Hiccup throughout this chapter, lets return to him one final time! Here's his full character arc in action:

1. Hiccup begins his positive arc suffering from a lack of self-worth. He struggles to live up to the "Viking ideal," but his small stature and intellectual disposition don't match up with that goal. To try and prove himself, he acts cold and aggressive.

2. After shooting down a dragon, Hiccup can't bring himself to kill it, despite knowing that's what any other Viking would do. Instead, he hides the dragon and cares for it, slowly becoming its friend and naming it Toothless. Eventually, he realizes the other Vikings are wrong about dragons—and perhaps about his worth as a person as well. He hatches a plan to convince them dragons aren't evil, but he still bases his self-worth on their approval.

3. Finally, Hiccup proves he's completed his positive arc when he goes against his father's wishes, frees Toothless, and teaches the other kids to befriend dragons as well. He stands up to his father and demands his respect, and by doing so he finally helps the other Vikings see the truth—both about him and dragons. In the process, he saves not only Toothless, but his entire village.

Even if you weren't previously familiar with character arcs, you'll likely find that many members of your core cast—especially your protagonist—loosely follow one of these arcs already. After a lifetime of exposure to storytelling, you've undoubtedly absorbed some of these ideas, even if only subconsciously. After all, these basic arcs are universal to storytelling for a reason—they work. Readers want to see characters change as they're affected by your story, because it gives your conflict a real, lasting impact within the lives of your cast. More importantly, it mirrors the natural growth and struggle we all experience in our own lives, making your characters feel even more alive to your readers.

Of course, since this is so important to your story, don't be afraid to take your time outlining your protagonist's arc. If you get stuck on any of the twelve questions you need to answer, I encourage you to move on to the next one. You can always return to the problematic question later on, and who knows—as you continue exploring your protagonist's character arc, the right answer may come to you naturally.

Additionally, as you work through these questions, feel free to write and rewrite different ideas in your protagonist's character profile until you hit on one that works.

What About Your Core Cast?

With your character sheet complete and your protagonist's profile done, you've finished all of your official goals for Day Six—congratulations!

Still, there may be some big gaps linger over the characters you've created in your draft outline. Specifically, think about your other core characters. While your protagonist will always have an arc of some kind, the characters around them don't have to. Yet, many of them may be perfect fits for having rich, intriguing arcs. The questions is, which ones?

Ultimately, deciding which of your core characters need arcs will be personal to your story. There's no right or wrong here, so you'll want to carefully consider which characters would benefit the most from having an arc. For instance, Chewbacca and Princess Leia are definitely core cast members in *Star Wars: A New Hope*. However, neither of them have distinct character arcs. That's ok, and doesn't detract from how great they are in that story! On the other hand, Luke Skywalker obviously has a character arc in *A New Hope,* but Han Solo does as well. Darth Vader even gets his own arc across the original trilogy.

Usually the characters most suited for having arcs of their own be the ones that start out with major flaws, since they naturally have the most potential for growth and change. You might also ask yourself who among your cast will play the biggest role next to your protagonist. These will almost always be your core cast members, which is yet another reason why we highlighted them earlier on—you really will reference that character sheet a lot!

Ultimately, whether you create one character with an arc or ten is up to you. Either way, you'll follow the same process as you did for your protagonist. Answer the questions we discussed above, and then create an individual profile for that character using the format we outlined.

By now, your draft outline should have:

- Your one to two sentence premise
- A short list covering the basics of your story
- A one or two paragraph story summary
- A list of 20+ potential scenes separated into beginning, middle, and end with brief paragraphs describing each group
- A paragraph covering basic rules and facts about your story's world

- A scene timeline (kept separate from your draft outline)
- **A single, alphabetical character sheet outlining your entire cast**
- **An in-depth character profile for your protagonist**

By now, your draft outline <u>might</u> have:

- Notes about your original inspiration
- A longer paragraph describing your full, high-concept idea
- A small group of "Undecided" scenes
- A photo of your day five timeline
- **Character profiles for any other characters with character arcs**

The Goals of Day Six

Since this chapter was so intense, I'll keep this portion brief.

While tackling today's goals, I hope you took the time to take breaks when needed. Sometimes it really can be beneficial to step away from your outline for a few minutes, allowing you to return with a clearer perspective. This will continue to be true as we get into tomorrow and start dealing with story structure and your story's plot. If you ever get stumped by your goals going forward, give yourself permission to take a break.

All of your hard work will come to fruition soon, so stick with it. After all, there are just a few more days before you reach the finish line!

Tomorrow your characters will help us create your story's

plot, but for now, here are the goals you've completed for Day Six:

1. List all of your characters alphabetically, and then mark your core cast members from that list.
2. Expand this list into your character sheet, filling in as much information as you can for each character.
3. Create a detailed character profile for your protagonist.
4. Repeat this in-depth profile for any other core characters you choose.

On to Day Seven!

7

DAY SEVEN: SIX ELEMENTS OF STRUCTURE

AS I PROMISED YESTERDAY, Day Seven will be all about applying structure to your story.

You see, story structure comes with some pretty significant benefits. Not only does it prevent your story from stagnating by providing clear points of transition, but it can—if used well—create a powerful sense of catharsis for your readers. All the elements of your story, from your characters to your scenes, should eventually come together within some kind of basic, structural framework. The final result will be a novel readers simply can't put down.

However, as was the case with character arcs, there's no way we can cover every aspect of structure here. Not only are there many types of story structure to choose from, but each type has a huge amount of nuance and complexity within it. Everything from episodic structure, to three and five act structures, to the Hero's Journey—yeah, you can see why people write volumes about this topic alone. As a result, today's take on story structure will be an abbreviated one.

Still, the elements we cover here should give you everything you need to understand basic structure and apply it to your novel. After all, the real key to mastering story structure is to use it while still honoring your original ideas. While many writers are wary of story structure for fear it will dictate their story to them, today's goals will only refine the story you've created—not replace it.

The Basics of Story Structure

Story structure is much like character development in that it involves a lot of technical terms, but can still be boiled down into a few essential parts.

At their core, story structures are culturally recognized ways of telling stories based on a clear set of plot points—plot points simply being scenes meant to fulfill a specific role in their respective structure. For you as a writer, these structures help you ensure every scene in your novel flows towards a clear end goal, slowly building towards key moments of change that shape the conflict of your story. The result is a novel that's deeply compelling and cathartic for your readers.

While there are many types of story structure out there, the one you're probably most familiar with is the Three Act Structure. This is the structure most common in Western storytelling and is basically standard for Hollywood movies. However, you can still find the framework of the Three Act Structure in almost all Western media, no matter how experimental. You may even find that your scene timeline loosely follows the Three Act Structure already, making it even easier to incorporate.

Since the Three Act Structure is both widely used and fairly easy to understand, it'll be the focus of this chapter. Of course, before you can start applying it to your story, we'll need to define it first!

For starters, each of the three acts in the aptly named Three Act Structure will serve a distinct purpose for your novel:

- **Act 1 (Setup):** Act 1 comprises the first quarter of your story and is all about preparing your cast for the journey ahead. This is where you'll introduce your setting, protagonist, and the main conflict they'll be facing.
- **Act 2 (Confrontation):** Act 2 forms the bulk of your story, around 50%. All the adventures, twists, and turns happen here, giving you time to flesh out your characters, backstories, and settings. Most importantly, Act 2 contains a major turning point where your protagonist shifts from reacting to the conflict to actively trying to resolve it thanks to the new skills and knowledge they've gained thus far.
- **Act 3 (Resolution):** Act 3 is the final quarter of your novel and sees the conflict come to its end. Here your protagonist and antagonist will have their final confrontation. Once you resolve the conflict of your story, you'll have a moment to hint at the future and explain what happens after your protagonist's journey is over (or set up a sequel, if you're planning one).

There are also a total of six major plot points you'll want to account for, two in each Act:

———

The Hook:

This is the scene that opens your story. It's designed to catch your reader's attention and encourage them to keep reading by introducing a unique aspect of your world or characters.

The First Plot Point:

This is the moment your story really begins, and it's also when Act 1 ends. Your protagonist has spent Act 1 learning about the conflict they're about to face, and here they'll finally become fully involved in the events of your story thanks to a pivotal decision they'll make.

The Midpoint:

This is the next major turning point of your story. Your Midpoint marks the halfway point of your novel and sees your protagonist face a major challenge. By overcoming this challenge they'll gain new skills or knowledge that will allow them to start actively shaping the events of your story. From here on out, they have a plan for resolving the conflict, even if that plan might fail later.

The Third Plot Point:

This plot point marks the end of Act 2 and is a harsh reality check for your protagonist. Here they'll suffer a major defeat at the hands of your antagonist, throwing their previous plans into disarray. This will be their lowest moment, when they feel like they've lost everything.

In the following scenes, they'll need to reflect on their goals in order to recommit to the journey ahead.

The Climax:

This is the final confrontation between your protagonist and antagonist. It may be a major battle, a confession of love, or a heated argument. Whatever it is, your protagonist will need to draw on all the skills, knowledge, and alliances they've gained throughout your story if they want to succeed. Alternatively, they may fail.

The Resolution:

These are the last few scenes of your story, meant to show your readers the final effects of your Climax. Whether your protagonist succeeded or failed in their quest, here you'll take a moment to say some final goodbyes and show what your story's world will look like going forward. You may also lay the groundwork for sequels here.

———

You can see this basic structure outlined in the graph below.

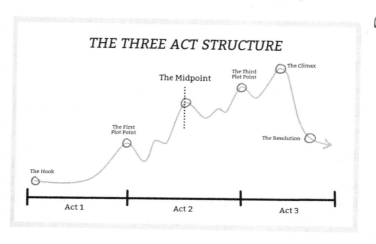

THE THREE ACT STRUCTURE

The Climax

The Third
Plot Point

The Midpoint

The First
Plot Point

The Resolution

The Hook

Act 1   Act 2   Act 3

This rising line represents the increasing tension as your story and its conflict progress. Likewise, the four major spikes at the First Plot Point, Midpoint, Third Plot Point, and Climax are because of the pivotal nature of those scenes—they'll naturally be more intense and involved than other scenes in your story. Similarly, the smaller valleys in this line are caused by the various scenes that occur between your six major plot points. More intense moments raise the line, while calmer periods of reflection lower it.

However, regardless of these dips, you can see that the overall trend is one of increasing tension leading up to the Climax. Every scene in your story should build towards the final confrontation in some way, no matter how subtle. Finally, once the Climax is over, your story settles into the Resolution, where readers see the aftermath of the Climax.

To help illustrate this structure in action, here's the plot of *Star Wars: A New Hope* broken down using these six major plot points:

————

The Hook:

Darth Vader intercepts Princess Leia's ship in search of stolen plans for the Death Star. However, Princess Leia sneaks them out of his grasp with the help of R2-D2.

The First Plot Point:

Upon returning home with Obi-Wan, Luke finds that Stormtroopers have killed his aunt and uncle. Now with a personal reason to hate the Empire, Luke joins Obi-Wan and the two set out in search of Princess Leia.

The Midpoint:

While searching for Alderaan, a tractor beam pulls the Millennium Falcon aboard the Death Star. The group must now escape, made even more complex when they realize Princess Leia is also on board.

The Third Plot Point:

Obi-Wan sacrifices himself in a battle with Darth Vader to buy Luke and his friends enough time to escape the Death Star. Luke is powerless as he watches Darth Vader kill his mentor and his last connection to home.

The Climax:

As the Death Star approaches the Rebel base, Luke and the other Rebel pilots scramble to destroy it. With Han Solo's help and his own trust in the Force, Luke blows up the Death Star.

Unknown to the Rebels, Darth Vader narrowly escapes.

The Resolution:

The movie ends during a large ceremony where Princess Leia honors Han and Luke for their role in helping destroy the Death Star.

————

What's interesting about the Three Act Structure is that it also overlaps with key moments of your characters' arcs. In fact, you can actually see how the major turning points in the three types of character arcs line up with the six plot points of the Three Act Structure. Check out this graph:

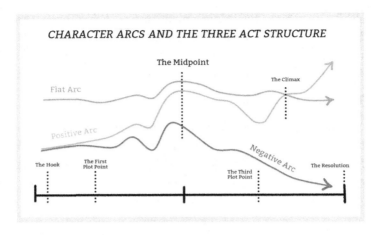

CHARACTER ARCS AND THE THREE ACT STRUCTURE

Your protagonist starts their inner journey at the same time they start their outer journey during The First Plot Point. Likewise, their emotional turning point happens alongside the turning point of your story—the Midpoint. They face their biggest setback at the Third Plot Point and finally prove whether or not they can overcome their inner flaw at the Climax. By the Resolution, you should be showing off the effects of their growth (or lack of growth) as a character, just like you should be showing the aftermath of your story's conflict.

Of course, all this talk of plot points and scenes might be getting confusing. What's the real difference between the two, or are they just different words for the same thing?

Well, no—plot points *are* a bit different from scenes.

Scenes, like we talked about on Day Four, are simply the individual events that make up your novel. Plot points, on the other hand, are the specific structural moments we just discussed above. Though most plot points will only contain a

single scene, some will need multiple scenes to fulfill their
unique requirements.

This is why we've been talking a lot about scenes in previous
chapters, but haven't yet talked about plot.

These six plot points are the foundation of your story's plot,
and it won't be fully formed until they're in place. Despite
common misconception, the scenes of your story and your
plot simply aren't the same thing, because plot is dependent
on your story's structure—in fact, it *is* your structure. Only
once you've combined these six points with the scenes from
your timeline will you have created the basic framework of
your plot. Fortunately, today is when we'll finally tackle this
next major element of your outline.

Outlining Your Plot

Now that we've established the basic ideas behind the Three
Act Structure, we can begin creating the plot of your own
novel. To do this, we'll be returning to your index cards, so
spread them out like you did on Day Five, making sure to
keep them in chronological order.

You'll also want to reference the conflict you wrote down on
Day Four. Since your whole plot revolves around this main
conflict, having it clearly defined and in the forefront of your
mind will make it much easier to identify which scenes fit
which plot points. After all, these scenes will be the ones
with the greatest impact on your conflict.

Of course, your story's conflict might have evolved over the
last few days. You'll have expanded on your original story a
lot by now, so it's worth taking a moment to reassess your
conflict and boil it back down to its core idea.

To do this, we'll rewrite your story's conflict as a question. In creative writing circles, this is referred to as the Dramatic Question, and is simply an expression of your story's most fundamental conflict. Here are some well-known Dramatic Questions you might be familiar with:

- Will Frodo destroy the One Ring?
- Will Luke defeat the Death Star?
- Will Katniss survive the Hunger Games?
- Will Moana restore Te Fiti's heart?

And here's the Dramatic Question for my own story:

- Will Varya stop the Soviets from starting WWIII?

This Dramatic Question is what your readers will ask while reading your novel, and it should be what you answer through your Climax. It may be the same as the conflict you originally created on Day Four, but it's just as likely that it will have evolved since then. Whatever it is, make sure it sums up the core conflict your protagonist will face.

Once you have your own Dramatic Question written down, you can begin setting up the rest of your plot. Start by writing down the six plot points we discussed previously, each on their own index card:

- The Hook
- The First Plot Point
- The Midpoint
- The Third Plot Point
- The Climax
- The Resolution

If you need to, feel free to write the definition of each plot point on their index card as well.

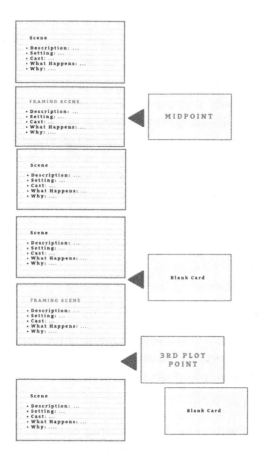

These six plot points will ultimately form the tent poles of your story, holding up every other scene in between. The rest of your story should follow a smooth series of cause and effect between these points, so you'll be using these index cards as markers that you can insert into the appropriate point on your timeline.

This is where today's real challenge begins—you'll need to go back through your timeline using these new index cards and figure out which of the scenes you've created best fit the various plot points of your story's structure.

Fortunately, it's likely that a large chunk of your timeline will match up closely with the Three Act Structure already, only needing small changes to existing scenes. Still, you'll inevitably find that some of these plot points don't have a corresponding scene at all. This means you'll need to introduce new blank cards to your timeline, both to fulfill various plot points and to patch up any holes you find in your newly created plot.

Here are a few tips for matching each card to your scenes:

———

The Hook:

This scene should occur right at the beginning of your story, preferably before any other scenes. It needs to introduce a unique aspect of your story that will intrigue readers.

The First Plot Point:

This scene will occur about a quarter of the way into your timeline, and is where your protagonist's adventure really begins. In it, they'll need to make a decision that forces them to get involved with your story's conflict. After this scene they may leave to a new location or otherwise experience a major shift in their situation.

They're moving away from their previous, ordinary life and into the unknown.

The Midpoint:

Look for this scene right in the middle of your timeline—it should be a turning point for both your protagonist and your story's conflict.

Your protagonist will need to prove they're learning and growing in order to handle a major challenge they'll face here, and if they succeed they'll be rewarded with new knowledge, tools, or skills. The scenes after your Midpoint will see your protagonist shift towards actively pursuing the conflict of their story.

The Third Plot Point:

You'll find this scene around three quarters of the way into your story. Here your protagonist will experience their darkest moment, both emotionally and physically. They'll suffer a huge defeat, and it will seem like all of their plans have failed. This is a time for them to question themselves and the journey they've been on.

The Climax:

This will probably be the easiest scene to spot in your timeline, because it's where all of your story's characters and conflicts come together one final time.

Here, your protagonist will use everything they've learned to overcome the antagonist and resolve your story's conflict in their favor. The outcome of this plot point will seal both the fate of your protagonist as well as the fate of the world and characters around them.

The Resolution:

These scenes will come after your Climax, marking the end of your story, and this is where you'll show what the world looks like after the Climax is over. What has changed, both about your protagonist and their world?

This is also when you'll say your final goodbyes to your characters and hint at what their lives will be like now that the conflict is over. Importantly, this plot point can consist of multiple scenes.

––––––

These tips should be you pretty far, but if you need a little extra boost, here's what my story's plot might look like based on this structure:

––––––

The Hook:

Varya is at the tail end of a mission when she finds herself under pursuit by a group of armed security forces. She manages to lose them in a crowd, but finds that one is harder to shake than the others. She swiftly kills the man in a nearby alley before slipping away, unnoticed by his allies.

The First Plot Point:

Kostya—the leader of the Soviet KGB—calls Varya into a private meeting where she is offered the top position on a secret mission meant to start World War III. Desperate to please him and rise in the ranks of the organization, she agrees. She'll do whatever it takes.

The Midpoint:

After Kostya decides Varya is dragging her feet, he sends other Soviet agents to attack her adoptive family. However, Varya protects them, suddenly realizing she's become more invested in their safety than in completing her mission. From here on out, she becomes Kostya's enemy.

The Third Plot Point:

Varya's adoptive family discovers her original mission after she's caught by US agents. She's put in a high security prison and her family denounces her. Soon after, she learns that Kostya is the one who sold her out.

The Climax:

Varya confronts Kostya, and during the exchange he reveals his personal motivation for targeting her adoptive family. Varya's adoptive parents also see the truth and forgive her. They work together, ultimately killing Kostya and alerting the targeted nuclear facility before WWIII starts.

The Resolution:

Varya's information is wiped from all databases, and she and her new family move away from their old town. However, they're happy together, and make plans for the new life they hope to lead.

———

By the end of this process, all of your plot points should be placed within your scene timeline and you should have anywhere from thirty-five and forty-five scenes in total, if not a few more.

Of course, less than thirty-five scenes can be ok, depending on your story. Still, if you find your final timeline has significantly less than thirty-five scenes, think hard about whether you've fully explored your story's idea. Most genres sit comfortably in that thirty-five to forty-five scene range, though there are certainly exceptions!

Updating Your Draft Outline

Once you've incorporated these six plot points into your timeline, you can record this newly formed plot in your draft outline. Fortunately, this step is fairly simple.

Returning to your draft outline, all you need to do is write down each of these six plot points in a list below your Dramatic Question. Then, record their corresponding scene(s) next to them. Add all of the information from those scenes' index cards to this list as well.

This is also a good time to do some other general cleanup of your timeline. Now that you know the six major plot points of your story, go through the rest of your scenes and mark any that contain important foreshadowing for these later moments. You may also want to review any of the notes and changes you made to your scenes, to ensure everything still works chronologically. Finally, gather your index cards in their correct, chronological order, maintaining any of the changes you've made. We'll need to pull them out a few final times in the coming days, so you'll want to keep your timeline intact and organized.

Once you've added all of your plot point cards to your larger scene timeline, simply stack them in order and store them the same way you did before.

By now, your draft outline should have:

- Your one to two sentence premise

- A short list covering the basics of your story
- A one or two paragraph story summary
- A list of 20+ potential scenes separated into beginning, middle, and end with brief paragraphs describing each group
- A paragraph covering basic rules and facts about your story's world
- A scene timeline (kept separate from your draft outline)
- A single, alphabetical character sheet outlining your entire cast
- An in-depth character profile for your protagonist
- **A list of your story's six plot points with their corresponding scenes**

By now, your draft outline <u>might</u> have:

- Notes about your original inspiration
- A longer paragraph describing your full, high-concept idea
- A small group of "Undecided" scenes
- A photo of your day five timeline
- Character profiles for any other characters with character arcs
- **A photo of your updated day seven timeline with plot points added**

The Goals of Day Seven

When dealing with story structure, there tends to be two opposing camps. One side structures their stories to the letter, going so far as to scrap their best ideas if they don't perfectly match their chosen structure. On the other end of the spectrum, many writers refuse to touch story structure at all for fear it will constrain their creativity.

However, as with so many other things in life, a balanced approach is best. I mentioned this in passing during today's introduction, but it felt too important not to reiterate once more—while you shouldn't be beholden to story structure, you also can't ignore its benefits.

Throughout today's goals, parts of your story may not have perfectly fit the six plot points of the Three Act Structure. Perhaps your Midpoint happened sixty percent through your novel rather than fifty percent, or maybe your protagonist didn't suffer a physical defeat at the Third Plot Point, but rather experienced a personal revelation. That's ok. In the end, preserving the core of your ideas can be worth bending the rules.

Story structure is an excellent tool for creating a novel that connects with your readers, and it can help you avoid some of the most common mistakes writers make. By following this framework, you ensure your story comes together with a satisfying conclusion, full of impactful moments along the way. After all, we wouldn't have spent an entire day applying structure to your novel if it wasn't worth the time.

However, if your plot doesn't perfectly fit the template we discussed, that's still ok. So long as you're confident your story is at its best, you'll be just fine.

Tomorrow we'll take your story to its final level, but for now, here are the goals you've completed for Day Seven:

1. Rewrite your conflict as a Dramatic Question.
2. Apply the six plot points of the Three Act Structure

to the scenes in your timeline, adding or changing scenes as needed.

3. Record this newly created plot in your draft outline.
4. Complete some general cleanup of your timeline before storing your index cards in their new order.

On to Day Eight!

8

DAY EIGHT: WHERE IT ALL COMES TOGETHER

YESTERDAY WE DISCUSSED QUITE a few elements of story structure, but today we're going to be taking that one step further. You see, though you have your story's plot in place, there's still another piece of the story structure puzzle you need to consider—your scenes.

As you might remember, scenes are essentially micro novels, following many of the same structural patterns we discussed yesterday. They start out with a clear goal, follow your characters through various challenges, are eventually resolved, and end with a new goal. Your next scene picks up that new goal, continuing the pattern in an unbroken chain until the final moments of your story.

With all the new elements you've created since Day Five—everything from characters to plot points—your scenes will already be in need of some cleanup, making this the perfect time to incorporate a more purposeful, cyclical structure. Rather than thinking of your scenes as just a string of chronological events, today you'll start to uncover the cause and effect that binds them all together.

Best of all, you'll end today with a complete, cohesive story on your hands—so let's get started!

Action Versus Reaction

Before you pull out your draft outline and index cards for today, we need to lay some groundwork around scenes.

As I mentioned above, scenes function like miniature novels in their own right. Just like every novel has a structure, your scenes will as well, with the major difference being that scenes follow an abbreviated structure. This structure is made up of six basic parts:

Scene Structure [handwritten annotation]

action [handwritten annotation]

- **Goal:** Your characters are pursuing a goal.
- **Challenges:** They face various conflicts while trying to reach that goal.
- **Outcome:** There's an outcome, either positive or negative.

reaction [handwritten annotation]

- **Reaction:** Your characters react to that outcome.
- **Reflection:** They consider their options going forward.
- **Decision (New Goal):** They make a decision, forming a new goal and beginning the cycle again.

These six parts create a natural ebb and flow in the pace and tension of your story, but more importantly, they form a clear through line between each scene in your novel. Since every scene begins and ends with a new goal, it's linked to the ones around it, forming a smooth chain of events.

This scene structure is also split into Action and Reaction phases, which help distinguish the specific purpose of each half of your scenes.

To start things off, the Action phase is what you might traditionally think of as a scene, and it contains the Goal, Challenges, and Outcome. It's all about your characters moving towards their goals, facing down enemies, forming alliances, and getting into trouble. At the end, they've either achieved their goal as they had hoped to, achieved it with unintended consequences, failed to achieve it outright, or achieved something else entirely.

What follows is the often less understood Reaction phase. In this phase, your characters get the chance to process what they've just experienced through the Reaction, Reflection, and Decision. Here they'll need to react to what's just happened, followed by a period of reflection. What're their options? Why did they succeed or fail? How do they feel about this, and what will they do now? Whatever they decide, this forms their new goal, which will be picked up in the next scene.

Overall, this Reaction phase doesn't need to be long, and the Action phase will usually make up the bulk of your scenes.

Most Reaction phases are only a paragraph or two, though some are as short as a sentence, while others occasionally span entire monologues. Usually the Reaction phase will be longest after major events within your story. There's more for your characters to process, after all!

Fortunately—as with many of this past week's goals—using a

template will make accounting for each of part of your various scenes much easier. Remember how we left the blank side of your index cards open? On these blank sides, you'll end up having:

- The single phrase you wrote back on Day Five.
- Goal:
- Challenges:
- Outcome:
- Reaction:
- Reflection:
- Decision:

This template will form the basic framework we'll use to connect your scenes together.

However, before we can begin filling in this template, there's one final thing you'll need to remember about *every scene* in your novel: they must either advance your plot or elaborate on something meaningful about your characters. If they don't fulfill one of these roles, you'll either need to change them or cut them outright.

While a select few scenes will be utility scenes—designed only to get your characters from point A to B—no scenes should be superfluous, and the best scenes will affect both your plot and characters. This is why purposefully creating the Action/Reaction split is so helpful. By doing so, you're ensuring each scene pulls double duty and impacts both aspects of your story, giving it far more meaning in the process. Action is all about your plot, while Reaction gives you time to focus on your characters.

Returning to Your Index Cards

With this basic understanding of scene structure taken care of, you can pull out your draft outline and index cards. Take a moment to spread them out in order, as always.

Your main task for today is to go through your timeline, filling out the six parts of each scene based on the template we laid out above.

> **A Quick Note:** If you've been outlining your novel digitally, this may be the best time to move your scenes from their index cards to your draft outline itself. You'll need to move these filled out scenes to your Master Outline tomorrow, which means a lot of rewriting if you don't have the luxury of copying and pasting. On the other hand, if you plan to keep your Master Outline on paper, you won't need to worry about this.

This is where your outline truly crosses into the territory of becoming a first draft in its own right. In fact, many of the decisions you'd normally make while writing your first draft will instead be made here, but in a fraction of the time—and with a fraction of the frustration. Since you have the benefit of reworking scenes at a glance, you can keep experimenting until they all slot comfortably together, saving you quite a few headaches and rewrites later on.

So, at the end of this process, each scene in your timeline should look something like this:

———

The Town Fair

- **Goal:** Contact her superiors on schedule.
- **Challenges:** Varya's adoptive family takes her to the town fair, and she's constantly interrupted by the various people there.
- **Outcome:** Varya gets in touch with her superiors, but is caught at the end by her adoptive mother.
- **Reaction:** Anxiety—she worries her adoptive mother might catch on to what she was doing.
- **Reflection:** She decides her adoptive mother is too naïve and brushes it off. She has her next target, so now she simply needs to follow her instructions and prevent further delays.
- **Decision:** Complete her next mission.

———

At its core, this is really that simple. Of course, I don't want to discount how challenging this task can be.

Today's goals are all about sitting down and committing to the hard work of drafting your story scene by scene. You'll likely find yourself filling out a scene, only to go back and change parts of it after working on a later one. To make this easier, use a pencil as much as possible and don't be afraid to jot down notes to return to later if you get stuck.

Similar to many of the goals earlier in the challenge, this is a lot like putting together a jigsaw puzzle. For this reason, I recommend completing your scenes in chronological order wherever you can, or at least creating your characters' goals chronologically. As you go, you'll be coming up with new goals at the end of each scene, and those goals should directly flow into the following scenes. Fortunately, that can actually make this task a lot easier. With a clear goal established, you simply need to provide challenges and decide on an outcome. From there, it's a matter of considering how your characters would react and what their followup goal would be—rinse and repeat.

Some Final Elements to Consider

Though it may seem strange on the surface, there's a reason I've saved today's goals until so late in the challenge.

Not only should you have a strong idea of your plot and a timeline of scenes to work with by now, but you should also have a variety of fleshed out characters to consider. All of them will should their own unique personalities and desires, meaning you can truly consider how they would react to the events of each of your scenes. These reactions and their broader goals for your story will ultimately morph into their specific scene by scene goals.

Of course, once you've established those goals, it's your job as the author to make achieving them difficult for your characters. It's rarely interesting to read about someone who accomplishes something with no challenge involved. The things we struggle for are the things we learn from the most, and your characters are no different. This will often come in the form of physical obstacles or enemies, but it could also be a mental roadblock they must overcome. Your characters may even have opposing goals, and this can be a great catalyst for conflict in its own right. When two allies want to tackle a problem in different ways, they'll not only fight between each other, but will often make achieving anything more difficult for the both of them.

Regardless of how you create them, make sure you have at least one meaningful challenge in each scene. As you encounter scenes that no longer work based on these new requirements, either rework them, remove them, or replace them with something new.

By now, your draft outline <u>should</u> have:

- Your one to two sentence premise
- A short list covering the basics of your story
- A one or two paragraph story summary
- A list of 20+ potential scenes separated into beginning, middle, and end with brief paragraphs describing each group
- A paragraph covering basic rules and facts about your story's world
- A scene timeline (kept separate from your draft outline)
- A single, alphabetical character sheet outlining your entire cast
- An in-depth character profile for your protagonist
- A list of your story's six plot points with their corresponding scenes

By now, your draft outline <u>might</u> have:

- Notes about your original inspiration
- A longer paragraph describing your full, high-concept idea
- A photo of your day five timeline
- Character profiles for any other characters with character arcs
- A photo of your updated day seven timeline with plot points added
- **All six parts of a scene filled out for each scene in your timeline**

The Goals of Day Eight

In the end, how in-depth your final scenes are is largely up to you. You may have jotted down a brief sentence for each part of your template, or you may have written an entire paragraph—both of these options are equally valid.

However, there are still some things to keep in mind, no matter how brief your final scenes are. I know I mentioned this previously, but it bears repeating: each scene you write should have a clear goal in mind. This will usually be a goal personal to your protagonist, since they're the focal point of your story, but it may also be one of their allies' goals or a goal given to them by another character. Regardless of its origins, this goal defines every other element of its scene, and will likely determine the goals of following scenes as well—meaning you don't want to ignore it.

You'll also want to periodically review your timeline. Make sure to look through it one final time after you think you've finished for the day, to ensure everything still flows logically together. After all, as you fill in your scenes you don't want to break something you set up earlier on.

Likewise, try to keep your story's plot in mind whenever you make changes to your scenes. Every scene in your novel needs to build towards your Climax in some form, as well as the various plot points along the way. There's a lot to consider here, but your plot is the perfect framework to help guide you. Don't be afraid to lean on it when needed!

Finally, consider your characters. Are the decisions they're making consistent with who they are as people? Are they growing and evolving as they experience new things and face new challenges? You want your characters to feel at home in

or not, if that's conflict or part of the conflict

your story's <u>world</u>, and paying careful attention to their reactions and behavior is the best way to do so.

Ultimately, all of this editing is a natural part of outlining your novel. Many of these edits would have been inevitable, cropping up later on during your second and third drafts if you didn't take care of them now. While difficult and time intensive, completing these now should help you end today confident that you have an airtight story on your hands.

In my opinion, that's well worth the work!

Tomorrow we'll finally form your Master Outline, but for now, here are the goals you've completed for Day Eight:

1. Set up your scene template using the six parts of a scene, either on each index card in your timeline or in your draft outline.
2. Begin filling out this template, specifically focusing on each scene's goal.
3. Jot down notes and rework scenes as needed until you feel confident that each scene flows comfortably into the next one.
4. Review your newly fleshed out scenes to ensure they're consistent with your characters and plot.

On to Day Nine!

9

DAY NINE: COMPLETING THE PICTURE

WE ALL HAVE someone in our lives who simply won't tolerate any less than our best, not out of a desire to be difficult, but because they know what we're capable of. For you, that may be a friend, editor, or coworker. Personally, one of my favorite college professors comes to mind.

Fortunately, these high standards are something we can apply to our own work, even without someone hanging over our shoulder to push us along. Today, you'll be doing exactly that for your novel, ensuring it meets your expectations on every level.

At this point, the story and characters you've outlined are probably good. In fact, they're probably great! However, there will always be things you miss the first time through. Over the last eight days you've undergone an intensive process, so it's only natural to lose things in the shuffle.

That's why Day Nine is acts as your final wrap up, giving you a chance to sift through your outline and patch up any last flaws and inconsistencies you may find.

Thanks to this simple round of proofreading, you'll be able to approach your first draft with confidence, knowing all of your storytelling ducks are in a row. Best of all, by the end of today you'll have completed your Master Outline!

Checking Things Over

Today is the last day of this challenge where you'll make any significant changes to your story. So, before you get to your Master Outline, you'll want to ensure every part of that story works within your final vision.

While you did a bit of this proofreading yesterday, that was mostly focused on plot. Here, you'll want to go step by step and review every aspect of your draft outline one last time.

————

Your Premise:

- Does your premise still sum up your story?
- Does it accurately cover your protagonist, their initial goal, and your story's main conflict?

Your World Building:

- Have the rules of your story's world changed?
- Is there anything you need to add or remove from this section?

Your Timeline:

- Do all of your scenes flow logically together?

- Does your story feel complete, or are there sections you still want to expand on?
- Alternatively, are there superfluous scenes you need to remove?
- Is all necessary foreshadowing accounted for in earlier scenes?
- Have you filled in all of your index cards?
- Have you ended up with roughly thirty-five to forty-five scenes?

Your Character Sheet:

- Have you covered every necessary character in your character sheet?
- Are there any characters you want to add or remove?
- Have you created character profiles for every character with an arc?
- Are all of your characters' goals clear?
- Are there any characters who need arcs, but don't have one?
- Are there any characters that have changed as you've developed your plot and timeline?

Your Plot:

- Are you happy with how your story fits within the six plot points of the Three Act Structure?
- Does your Dramatic Question properly capture your story's conflict?
- Does your story steadily raise the stakes and tension as you approach your final Climax?
- Do you resolve all of your loose story threads during your Climax and Resolution?

As you go, pay special attention to how these pieces work as a whole. The final question you should ask is: Is this a story you'd be excited to read? If the answer is a resounding "yes," you're in a good place!

Of course, it's natural to feel some doubt at this point, simply because we're always hardest on ourselves. However, Instead of letting this doubt get to you, make a point to cut yourself a little slack and set your nervousness aside. Give yourself credit where credit is due. You're on the second to last day of an intense challenge, you've accomplished a lot, and by the end you'll have even more to show for it! If you still feel in need of a second opinion, enlist a trusted friend and have them skim through your draft outline. You can even have them quiz you using the questions above if that will help you see your story more objectively.

By the time you're done reviewing your draft outline, you want to be completely comfortable with the story you've created. Once you are, it's finally time for your Master Outline to take shape.

Creating Your Master Outline

Throughout this challenge, you've been working through your story's most complex elements in your draft outline, but now it's time to refine that draft into something more cohesive.

Still, you may find yourself wondering why you can't just use your current outline as you write your first draft, and there are a few reasons.

To start, your draft outline acts as a paper trail, preserving each stage of your story's development. If you ever question why you made a certain decision or forget where your original inspiration came from, you can easily track that down in your draft outline. Plus, when you finally hold your finished novel in your hands, there's something cathartic about looking back over your original ideas and seeing the rough beginnings of what is now a polished piece of fiction.

Additionally, your Master Outline is a more streamlined version of your draft outline. When it comes time to write your first draft, you don't want to be flipping through pages of old and potentially outdated notes. Instead, you'll need a clear, organized roadmap to work from, and that's what this outline will ultimately be. By the end of today, it'll cover every element of your story in an easy to reference format, alongside a few important additions.

Thus, the first step in creating your Master Outline is pretty much the same as it was for your draft outline—you'll need to decide what to create it in.

Even if you created the entirety of your draft outline in a notebook or on your computer, think about whether that would be the best place for your Master Outline as well. Remember to consider ease of use, level of distraction, and your overall enjoyment. However, also keep in mind that this Master Outline is meant to be used as a reference *while* you're writing your first draft. Make sure that, whatever you create it in, it'll be intuitive for you to pull out and look through as you write.

With that issue decided on, open a new document or flip to a fresh page in your notebook. At the top, write down your story's working title and premise. From there, you'll want to fill out your story's conflict, your protagonist's personal struggle, and your Dramatic Question.

You should already know most of these by now—the only one that may trip you up is your protagonist's personal struggle, but this is simply their stake in the conflict. What do they stand to gain or lose, and what are they struggling to achieve?

When filling these in, leave a blank line beneath your premise, because we'll be coming back to add some extra information in a moment. Once you've finished this, the top of your Master Outline should look something like this:

———

Premise:

During the Cold War, a teenaged girl sets out as an undercover agent to spy on their adoptive family—a difficult mission, considering their adoptive parents are spies themselves.

(blank)

Conflict:

The leader of the KGB is trying to start World War III. Varya begins the story intent on helping him, but will soon turn on him to protect the family that views her as a traitor.

Dramatic Question:

Will Varya stop the Soviets from starting WWIII?

Protagonist's Personal Struggle:

Varya wants to gain respect from her boss by helping him spark a world war, but soon defects. From there she must reconcile what she's done with who she wants to be, all while struggling to repair the broken trust between her and her adoptive family.

————

These elements are meant to form a broad overview of what you've created, and will be there to remind you of each of the core elements of your story. This also makes this the perfect place to list notes about your worldbuilding, so add those right below this section.

Next, you'll want to create a more detailed breakdown of your plot and scenes by making your timeline something easier to reference. This will take the longest to set up of all the pieces of your Master Outline, but it will also be what you likely find yourself using the most while writing. Pull out your timeline, because you'll be using it a lot here.

To create this section, sum up the beginning (Act 1), middle (Act 2), and end of your story (Act 3), each in a single sentence. Leave plenty of space below these, anywhere from a few lines up to an entire page.

After you've finished these short sentences, you'll want to write a longer paragraph covering everything that happens during each portion of your story. These are essentially the summary paragraphs you created all the way back on Day Four, but updated to fit this final version. Once you've formulated these paragraphs, write them in their respective sections.

Finally, to finish this portion of your Master Outline, list each section's scenes beneath the appropriate paragraph. As you go, mark the ones that fulfill any of the various plot points we've covered. This portion of your Master Outline will look something like this, though your paragraphs and the list of scenes beneath them will be much longer for your own Master Outline:

———

Beginning (Act 1):

The leader of the KGB sends Varya on a special mission to gain access to the United States' nuclear arsenal.

> The story begins at the very end of one of Varya's missions, where she kills an armed security guard as he follows her through a crowd. Later on, Varya is brought to meet with her boss, the head of the Soviet KGB, and he offers her a secret mission. She accepts and, after some paperwork and a new identity, is put on a flight to America.

- Chase Scene - THE HOOK
- Returning to Base
- Praise From Above
- …
- An Important Offer - FIRST PLOT POINT

Middle (Act 2):

At first she dismisses them, but soon Varya finds herself protecting her adoptive family instead of going along with her original mission.

> Once in America, Varya meets her adoptive family at the airport. In an attempt to win her over they take her to their local town fair, but she spends the whole time trying to sneak away to contact her superiors back home. After receiving her next mission…

- Arriving in Her New Home
- The Town Fair
- ...
- A New Enemy - MIDPOINT
- Formulating Her Plan
- ...
- The Truth is Discovered - THIRD PLOT POINT

Ending (Act 3):

Varya regains the trust of her new family at the last moment, saving them and stopping WWIII all in one go.

> After coming to terms with what she's done, Varya decides she can't allow her new family to get hurt. She breaks out of prison and goes into hiding. As she uses her skills to hunt her old boss down, she realizes his plan to spark WWIII is about to begin...

- A Moment to Reflect
- Jailbreak
- Predator and Prey
- Finding Forgiveness
- The Final Confrontation - CLIMAX
- ...
- Leaving for a New Life - RESOLUTION

———

This is also when you'll need to make a decision about how you'll use your Master Outline. You can either list your scenes with only their short phrase, as I did above, or you can transfer all the information from each of your index cards to your Master Outline itself.

In that instance, you'll want to create a separate page covering all the details for your scenes, leaving this portion of your Master Outline with just the short phrases. This will make it much easier to search through at a glance.

Personally, I tend to keep my scenes on their index cards and pull out each card to reference as I write my first draft. However, I also write at home, so my cards are easily accessible from my desk drawer. If you like to write at coffee shops, libraries, or another public space, this may be less realistic for you. In that instance, it's probably worth the time to transfer your scenes to their own page within your Master Outline.

Finally, to finish the bulk of your Master Outline, you'll be recreating your character sheet and profiles.

This step is fairly simple, because it doesn't require you to create anything new. All you need to do is transfer your character sheet into your Master Outline itself. Make sure to preserve the alphabetical order of your characters' names and incorporate your various character profiles into the sheet as well.

By the end, this section of your Master Outline will be structured like this:

———

Name: Description...

- Goal
- Background
- Personality
- Flaws
- Other information

Varya:

The protagonist, a Soviet teen sent to spy on a family of US special operatives with access to important state secrets, she is the prodigy of the head of the Soviet KGB.

- **Goal:** Varya wants to rise in the ranks of the KGB and gain respect from her superiors.
- **Background:** Varya wasn't born a native Russian. She's actually from Georgia, a Soviet republic. As she got older, she was taught to idolize Russia. When her classmates protested Soviet control, she ratted them out, resulting in them being killed and her being rewarded with a job in the Soviet KGB as an operative. She's slowly risen in the ranks since that incident.
- **Personality:** Driven, determined, intelligent
- **Flaws:** Bottled-up, aggressive, quick to judge others
- **Struggle:** She believes people aren't worthy of respect unless they're useful
- **Lesson:** Everyone is worthwhile for their own unique reasons, herself included
- **Arc:** Yes - Positive Arc
- **Miscellaneous:** She borders on scrawny in appearance, but she's physically strong despite this. She's particularly proud of her ability to speak many languages.

Name: Description...

- Goal
- Background
- Personality
- Flaws

- Other information

———

I also strongly recommend highlighting your core character profiles within this sheet—just like you did in your draft outline—to make them easier to find at a glance. Again, your Master Outline is all about ease of reference!

The Finishing Touches

With that out of the way, you have the majority of your Master Outline complete. However, there is one final thing you'll want to incorporate—point of view.

Remember the blank line we left below your premise in your Master Outline? That's where this will ultimately live.

Put simply, point of view (often abbreviated POV)is the perspective your story is told from, and it plays a big role in how you'll write your final novel. There are four types of point of view that most fiction writers use:

———

First Person POV:

In this point of view, the narrator of your story is also one of the characters, usually the protagonist. They tell the entire story as "I did/thought/felt/saw/etc…" This means the story is limited to what the narrator experiences.

- **Example:** Harper Lee's *To Kill A Mockingbird*

Peripheral First Person POV:

This is the same as regular First Person point of view, except the narrator is not the protagonist. Instead, they're a secondary character, and the reader is limited to seeing and experiencing the protagonist's story through that peripheral narrator's experiences.

- **Example:** F. Scott Fitzgerald's *The Great Gatsby*

Limited Third Person POV:

Third Person point of view is where the narrator is not a character within your story. Instead, they tell the story as an outside observer, recounting it using he/she/they.

In a limited Third Person point of view specifically, the narrator is limited to telling the story based on the experiences of a single character, usually the protagonist. They can only guess at what other characters are thinking and feeling based on expressions and conversations, much like First Person point of view.

- **Example:** J. K. Rowling's *Harry Potter and the Chamber of Secrets*

Omniscient Third Person POV:

This point of view uses the same he/she/they pronouns as limited Third Person, but an omniscient narrator has access to every characters' thoughts and feelings, regardless of which character the story focuses on. This means they can discuss everything that's happening to every character within the story simultaneously.

- **Example:** Nathaniel Hawthorne's *The Scarlet Letter*

We've saved choosing one of these points of view until now, because first you needed a solid understanding of the story you wanted to tell. Now that you have that, you just need to decide how you as the author will tell your story.

In the end this will be personal to your novel, but as a general rule, both forms of First Person point of view are best for more intimate stories. This point of view connects your reader directly to your narrator and to their thoughts and feelings. On the other hand, Third Person point of view is more distant, and lets you follow the story much like you'd watch a movie.

Finally, Omniscient Third Person is a special case, more suited for complex stories with a large variety of characters to focus on. Of course, this makes it by far the most difficult to write as well. Either way, there's really no right or wrong here—it's ultimately up to you.

Once you've chosen your story's point of view, write it in the space beneath your premise. You've officially completed your Master Outline, and almost done with this challenge!

By now, your Master Outline should have:

- Your one to two sentence premise
- Your story's point of view
- A short description of your story's conflict and your protagonist's personal struggle
- Your Dramatic Question
- Notes about your story's world and worldbuilding
- An organized version of your timeline—split into beginning, middle, and end—with the appropriate scenes listed below each section

- A paragraph describing each section of your story
- Your complete character sheet in alphabetical order, with your core characters highlighted for reference purposes
- Your stack of index cards containing the full breakdowns of each scene in your story

The Goals of Day Nine

Throughout this challenge, I've talked a lot about what a valuable tool your Master Outline will end up being, but I haven't really gone into the specifics of why. You see, as you sit down to write your first draft, your Master Outline will become an invaluable roadmap.

Specifically, it should benefit your writing in a few ways:

———

General Support:

This is probably the most obvious role your Master Outline will play, but that doesn't make it any less important.

As you write, you'll need something to keep you moving forward in your story. By referencing your Master Outline as you finish each scene, you'll always know what's ahead of you, allowing you to create a story that flows comfortably into a single whole.

Understanding Characters:

Characters are one of the most difficult parts of writing any novel. They're naturally complex, just like real people. This is why working through their personalities and goals early on is so helpful.

Now, when you sit down to introduce a new character, your Master Outline will be able to tell you how they'll act and sound. As you get deeper into your story you'll also have an idea of how they'll grow and change as well.

Planning and Setting Goals:

Your Master Outline is a great tool for planning what you need to write and when.

Personally, I work best when I have deadlines to meet. It keeps me honest and makes it less likely I'll save my work until the last minute. By using your Master Outline, you can set goals for yourself based on how many scenes you want to write or when you want to finish each section of your story. There's no question how much needs to get done, you just need to decide when you want to finish it and how you want to split it between writing sessions.

Editing:

On the surface, this may seem like the least intuitive benefit of an outline. How does your Master Outline have anything to do with editing your later drafts?

Well, not only will having a Master Outline make your first draft better overall, but it'll make it easier to track down issues when you go to edit it. You'll already have an overview of your story on hand, so instead of shuffling through thousands of words to find a specific problem, you can quickly turn to your Master Outline for guidance.

Combating Doubt:

Finally, you'll inevitably feel some doubts while working on your first draft. You're setting out to tackle a big project, and that naturally comes with some anxiety.

However, by going through this challenge, you'll have your Master Outline always on standby to remind you that your story *works*. You won't need to wonder halfway through your draft whether everything will come together in the end—you already have proof it will.

So, whenever you're stuck, turn to your Master Outline. Somewhere inside, you should find what you need to keep writing!

———

Tomorrow you'll complete your final preparations before writing your first draft, but for now, here are the goals you've completed for Day Nine:

1. Go back over your draft outline using a series of questions and fix any final issues you may find.
2. Decide where you'll create your Master Outline.
3. Record your premise, an overview of your conflict, your worldbuilding, your plot and scenes, and your characters in your new Master Outline.
4. Choose a point of view for your story and add that to your Master Outline as well.

On to the final day!

10

DAY TEN: WHAT ABOUT TOMORROW?

TODAY IS an outlier within this challenge.

Over the past nine days, each set of goals you completed ramped up in intensity. Slowly but steadily you built the foundation of your novel, framed it with scenes, and finished it with a cohesive structure and cast. I can't say I meant for any day along the way to be relaxing—creating a truly compelling story is no walk through the park, after all.

Today, on the other hand, is all about rest.

No, seriously! The final day of this ten-day challenge *is* all about taking a break from the intense journey you just completed. While we have one or two small tasks left to take care of, they'll seem like nothing compared to the goals of previous days.

You see, if you're anything like I am, you'll be tempted to set strict goals as you sit down to write your first draft. After all, goals are how we make plans, and they discourage us from giving into the temptation of procrastination. Our goals give us a destination on the horizon, and that's a big deal.

However, just like this ten-day challenge only *technically* took nine days to complete, all of your goals need some mercy built in. As a friend once warned me, if you have ten days to write, plan to write for nine. That way, when one day takes longer than expected, you have a backup there to help keep you on track.

Unfortunately, I'll probably always be the person who sets extreme deadlines, but I don't want you to make the same mistakes. Committing to writing a novel is a huge test in its own right, so you want to give yourself the time you need to succeed. While we do have a few final tasks before we wrap up this challenge, I hope today will linger in your mind as a reminder to give yourself some mercy days as you tackle your next challenge—writing your novel.

Preparing for the Next Phase

While the challenge you've just completed was all about outlining on the surface, in reality, these ten days have been about preparing yourself to begin the first draft of your novel. The Master Outline you created yesterday was by far the biggest part of that, but it's not all you'll need.

Whether you begin writing your novel tomorrow or months from now, you'll need a supportive mental and physical environment for doing so, and the first step in creating that positive environment is having a workspace to call home.

If you've completed this challenge from your home office, at a well-worn desk, or in a comfy chair in your living room, you may think that's all you need. Task complete, right? In reality, creating a supportive workspace is less about where you write and more about how you use the space you're in.

No matter where you choose to write your first draft, you'll want it to think about these things:

————

Focus:

Much like I warned against creating your outline on your laptop if the Internet tends to distract you, you don't want to write a novel at the kitchen table if you have six cats, four dogs, and a gaggle of tiny humans running around your legs. Wherever you work, make sure it's somewhere you can concentrate, without too many distractions.

Comfort:

While noise is definitely distracting, being uncomfortable can be distracting in its own right. Finding a comfortable chair along with a desk or table that's at the right height for you can make a huge difference in your writing, simply because you've improved your posture and overall comfort.

Supplies:

Wherever you choose to write, you'll need easy access to the tools you like to use. Pens, pencils, paper, charging cables, books, sticky notes—no matter what your personal toolkit looks like, make sure you have everything you need set aside in your chosen workspace. This way you won't need to break your flow to find a pencil sharpener or get a glass of water.

Inspiration:

Your workspace should inspire you as much as possible. Try to find somewhere beautiful, or at least filled with things that make you feel happy and relaxed. Natural light, plants, color, and a good view can go a long way towards keeping your mind active and, most importantly, creative. Likewise, eliminate stressful clutter as best you can.

––––––––––

Of course, these four things are usually easier to fulfill when you have the same space to work in day after day, but they're just as doable if you work in a variety of locations.

You may write in a noisy coffee shop, but a pair of noise canceling headphones can be a simple way to help you concentrate on the work at hand. Likewise, keeping necessary notebooks, pencils, pens, and computer chargers with you will prevent you from needing to leave your chosen workspace, or put your writing on hold until later.

Fortunately, writing in new and interesting locations can often be the best thing for your inspiration. Even though I'm a writing hermit and concentrate best when writing at my kitchen table, some days I just need a change of scenery. Seeing the world through a different lens can energize your mind when you need it the most.

So, regardless of your ideal workspace, take a few minutes to gather the materials you'll need for writing. Clear the space of unnecessary distractions and set your tools out so they're ready and waiting for you. If you plan to commute to your writing space, gather your supplies in a bag or backpack so they're easy to carry with you.

With your workspace taken care of, it's time to turn to the mental side of writing. I promised your collection from Day Two would come up again and, though it took quite a while, now is finally the time!

Before moving on, look through your original collection and

pick out five to ten pieces to add to the end of your Master Outline. You can print out images and transcribe quotes or, if you've created your outline digitally, you can simply copy and paste them into the document. If you'd like to take this a step further, pick out a specific piece from your collection that represents the setting or tone of each plot point in your story and add it beneath those scenes in your Master Outline. Now, whenever you hit a roadblock, you can return to these bits of inspiration to get yourself back on track.

Of course, sometimes inspiration isn't what you'll need.

There will inevitably be a few times while writing your novel when you just want to give up, not because you don't know what to create, but because it's just gotten too hard. You have too much else to do, you're tired, you've had a long week at work—whatever it may be, there will always be a reason not to write.

Ultimately, these reasons are completely valid. It's up to you when the best time to write is, and there's no shame in taking a day off. However, no matter how valid they are, many writers never become authors simply because these reasons overwhelm them. They may dream of one day finishing a novel, but when push comes to shove, too many other things get in the way.

Sometimes, there's truly nothing you can do about this. There will be times when life demands your attention and when your novel has to wait for another day. Yet, just as often, what you may be missing is your Why:

- Why are you writing a novel to begin with?
- Why does this matter to you, so much so that you'd dedicate weeks of work to make it happen?
- Why do you care?

If you've gotten this far, you clearly have a good reason for doing so, something beyond "I just want to write a book." Perhaps you have an important story to tell, or maybe you want to leave something behind for the next generation. Maybe writing is therapy for you. There's really no right or wrong here.

Whatever your Why is, make sure you find it before you sit down to write your first draft. Take some time to consider what makes writing meaningful to you and then write your answer down where you'll always see it. Whether that's a sticky note above your desk or a short sentence at the top of your first draft, keep it close to your heart so you never have to wonder "why am I doing this?"

Stepping Into the Future

With all your preparations completed, I'm proud to say this challenge has officially come to an end.

You've accomplished a lot over the last ten days. Not only have you created a story from the ground up, but you've continued to stretch and strengthen it into something better and more expansive than you likely realized it could ever be. You've truly created the foundation of an excellent novel.

Now you stand at an important threshold. Whether you take the next step tomorrow or a year from now, all that's left to do is write.

Yet, you may find yourself surprised that, as you write your first draft, your story will continue to evolve. Ultimately, no matter how thorough we've been, your story will always have imperfections. You'll discover you've missed things, or you'll find sparks of inspiration that become entirely new scenes and characters, changing your story in exciting ways.

When the time comes to turn your draft into a finished work of fiction, you'll still find yourself tweaking your story and editing things both large and small.

All of this is just as it should be. The process of creating a living world full of people, places, and events is one that is never truly over. In many ways, that's the beauty of it— there's always more to discover.

In the end, the true value of the outline you've created over the last ten days is that it gives you confidence. You'll never have to doubt whether the foundation of this story you're trying to create is strong. With the hardest decisions behind you, ahead is the simple process of putting pen to paper. The next time you sit down to write you'll be starting your first draft, diving in to create the words and phrases that will eventually become your finished novel.

You have the tools you need to bring your story to life—now it's just a matter of doing so.

Tomorrow you'll begin the next phase of your novel, but for now, here are the goals you've completed for Day Ten:

1. Choose your writing space, and then prepare it with any supplies you'll need.
2. Add five to ten pieces from your collection to your Master Outline. Optionally, assign a piece to each scene in your timeline.
3. Discover your "Why," and then write it somewhere you'll always see it.
4. Begin writing your novel!

WHAT COMES NEXT?

With our time together at an end, I just wanted to say—thank you for taking on this challenge!

It's been an intense ten days, but I hope you're proud of the story you've created. Most of all, I hope you're excited to transform it into a finished novel in the weeks to come. Not only will your Master Outline be there to guide you through every step along your writing journey, but it will serve as a reminder that yes—you are capable of writing a novel!

Of course, you may still have questions, in which case I encourage you to reach out and send me an email.

When I'm not busy writing books like these and getting lost in my own fictional worlds, I run **The Novel Smithy**, a site dedicated to giving new writers the tools they need to create their dream novels.

Finally, if you enjoyed this book, leaving a review would not only help me, but other writers as well. Reviews are how readers find the books they're looking for, so I hope you'll take a moment to leave some honest feedback.

With that said, this book—and your outlining challenge—is officially complete!

Happy writing,

Lewis

JOIN THE LIBRARY!

Ever wish there was a library of resources built just for novelists? Well, guess what—there is!

Check out the **Novel Smithy Resource Library** and grab your **FREE Character Creation Workbook**.

https://thenovelsmithy.com/library/

ABOUT THE AUTHOR

Lewis Jorstad is a writer, author, and book coach, a lover of reading and travel, and a child at heart living in central Virginia. He hopes to visit every country in the world before he dies, but for now he spends his time teaching up-and-coming writers the skills they need to create compelling, successful novels—all from the comfort of his blue couch.

You can find more of his work over at **The Novel Smithy**:

https://thenovelsmithy.com/

THE COMPLETE TEN DAY OUTLINING PROCESS

If you need a reminder of the goals you've completed throughout this challenge, here they are in an easy to reference format:

Day One: Start With the Basics

1. Brainstorm an initial idea, either using one you already have or creating one for this challenge.
2. Expand on your initial idea until it fulfills the four requirements of a high-concept story.
3. Condense your idea into a one to two sentence premise that clearly outlines your main character, their initial goal, and your story's conflict.
4. Pick a medium and begin your draft outline by writing your new premise at the top.

Day Two: How to Find Your Inspiration

1. Gather 100 pieces of media (images, music, quotes, excerpts, et cetera…) that represent your story.
2. Separate this media into categories of your choice.
3. Sort through these categories and remove any items that no longer fit your story.
4. Write down your current vision of your story, along with any new ideas you've come up with.

Day Three: Questions for Exploring Every Angle

1. Create a set of ten questions based on your premise.
2. Answer each of these questions with two separate answers, and then highlight the sections of your answers you like the most.
3. Rewrite your ten highlighted answers in their own list and create a new question for each of them.
4. Repeat the above process for these new questions.
5. Write a one to two paragraph story summary based on the new information you've learned.

Day Four: The Start of Your Story's Scenes

1. Brainstorm a list of 20+ potential scenes that fulfill the various requirements of your story.
2. Divide these 20+ scenes into three groups—beginning, middle, and end.
3. Write a brief paragraph for each group describing what happens in that section of your story.
4. Create a short paragraph going over the rules of your

story's world and any important elements of worldbuilding you'll need to know later.

Day Five: Forming a Scene Timeline

1. Create index cards for each of your 20+ scenes.
2. Spread these index cards out on a large, flat surface and organize them in chronological order, adding blank index cards wherever you feel your story could be expanded upon.
3. Using a series of questions, fill out this timeline until you have 30+ scenes, leaving as few blank cards as possible.
4. Take a photo or otherwise mark the index cards in your timeline to reference later in the challenge.

Day Six: Creating the Character Sheet

1. List all of your characters alphabetically, and then mark your core cast members from that list.
2. Expand this list into your character sheet, filling in as much information as you can for each character.
3. Create a detailed character profile for your protagonist.
4. Repeat this in-depth profile for any other core characters you choose.

Day Seven: Six Elements of Structure

1. Rewrite your conflict as a Dramatic Question.
2. Apply the six plot points of the Three Act Structure

to the scenes in your timeline, adding or changing scenes as needed.

3. Record this newly created plot in your draft outline.
4. Complete some general cleanup of your timeline before storing your index cards in their new order.

Day Eight: Where Your Story Comes Together

1. Set up your scene template using the six parts of a scene, either on each index card in your timeline or in your draft outline.
2. Begin filling out this template, specifically focusing on each scene's goal.
3. Jot down notes and rework scenes as needed until you feel confident that each scene flows comfortably into the next one.
4. Review your newly fleshed out scenes to ensure they're consistent with your characters and plot.

Day Nine: The Complete Picture

1. Go back over your draft outline using a series of questions and fix any final issues you may find.
2. Decide where you'll create your Master Outline.
3. Record your premise, an overview of your conflict, your worldbuilding, your plot and scenes, and your characters in your new Master Outline.
4. Choose a point of view for your story and add that to your Master Outline as well.

Day Ten: What About Tomorrow?

1. Choose your writing space, and then prepare it with any supplies you'll need.
2. Add five to ten pieces from your collection to your Master Outline. Optionally, assign a piece to each scene in your timeline.
3. Discover your "Why," and then write it somewhere you'll always see it.
4. Begin writing your novel!

————

Your Complete Master Outline Should Have:

- Your one to two sentence premise
- Your story's point of view
- A short description of your story's conflict and your protagonist's personal struggle
- Your Dramatic Question
- Notes about your story's world and worldbuilding
- An organized version of your timeline—split into beginning, middle, and end—with the appropriate scenes listed below each section
- A paragraph describing each section of your story
- Your complete character sheet in alphabetical order, with your core characters highlighted for reference purposes
- Your stack of index cards containing the full breakdowns of each scene in your story

"Start writing, no matter what. The water does not flow until the faucet is turned on."

LOUIS L'AMOUR, AMERICAN NOVELIST AND SHORT-STORY AUTHOR

ALSO BY LEWIS JORSTAD

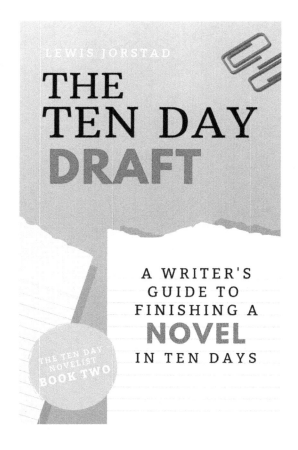

It's time to begin your next great adventure.

It's time to write a novel!

Made in the USA
Middletown, DE
12 September 2020

19535328R00096